WONDERFUL WORLD OF KNOWLEDGE

YEAR BOOK 1981

Disney's

Wonderful World of Knowledge

YEAR BOOK 1981

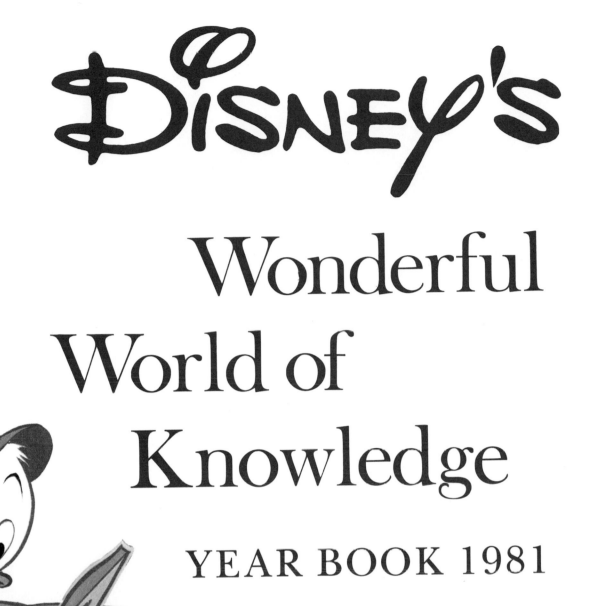

GROLIER ENTERPRISES, INC.
Danbury, Connecticut

ROBERT B. CLARKE   *Publisher*

WILLIAM E. SHAPIRO   *Editor in Chief*

FERN L. MAMBERG   *Executive Editor*

MICHÈLE A. McLEAN   *Art Director*

RICHARD SHAW   *Production Manager, Manufacturing*

ALAN PHELPS   *Assistant Production Manager*

· · · · · · · · · · · · · · · · · ·

HOWARD B. GRAHAM   *Senior Vice-President, Publishing*

BERNARD S. CAYNE   *Vice-President and Editorial Director*

HARRIET RIPINSKY   *Vice-President and Director of Manufacturing*

ISBN 0-7172-8156-6
The Library of Congress Catalog Card Number: 78-66149

CONTENTS

1980 AT A GLANCE

JANUARY 14.   Indira Gandhi was elected prime minister of India. She had held this position before, from 1966 to 1977. Her return as India's leader came after her party, the Congress Party, had won the most seats in parliamentary elections. ■ The U.N. General Assembly condemned the Soviet Union for intervening in Afghanistan. It called on the Soviet Union to withdraw its troops from that country. Starting the last week of December, 1979, the Soviet Union had sent thousands of troops into Afghanistan to help that country's pro-Soviet government put down Muslim tribes who were fighting a guerrilla rebellion.

JANUARY 25.   Abolhassan Bani-Sadr was elected president of Iran. But Ayatollah Ruhollah Khomeini remained the supreme ruler of the country.

JANUARY 28.   Six Americans escaped from Iran with the help of Canadian diplomats. The six were employees of the U.S. embassy in Teheran. They had fled the embassy when it was seized by Iranian militants on November 4, 1979. They eventually made their way to the Canadian embassy. The Canadians hid the Americans for almost three months. They then got them out of Iran with forged Canadian passports. Meanwhile, 53 Americans continued to be held hostage in Iran.

FEBRUARY 18.   In parliamentary elections in Canada, the Liberal Party won the most seats. Pierre Elliott Trudeau, head of that party, thus became prime minister once again. He replaced Joe Clark, who had been prime minister for nine months. Prior to that, Trudeau had been prime minister for eleven years.

MARCH 24.   Engineers finally capped Ixtoc 1, an oil well in the Gulf of Mexico. The well had blown out on June 3, 1979. Before being capped, it had spilled more than 3,000,000 barrels of crude oil into the Gulf. This was the largest oil spill in history.

APRIL 18.   Rhodesia, a former British colony, became the independent nation of Zimbabwe. Robert Mugabe became prime minister. Mugabe had led one of the major guerrilla groups that had long fought for black majority rule in Rhodesia.

APRIL 24.   A U.S. mission to rescue the American hostages in Teheran, Iran, ended in failure. The plan called for at least six Navy helicopters to fly at night to a remote spot in the desert southeast of Teheran. There they would meet transport planes carrying Army commandos, fuel, and supplies. The helicopters would ferry the commandos to a mountain hideout near Teheran. Then, under cover of darkness, the commandos would enter Teheran, storm the embassy, and free the hostages. The helicopters would carry the soldiers and hostages out. But the raid did not turn out as planned. Eight helicopters set out on the mission from an aircraft carrier near the Strait of Hormuz. But two developed trouble, so only six arrived at the rendezvous, where the transport planes were waiting. When yet another helicopter developed mechanical problems, the mission was called off, because five helicopters were too few to complete the operation. During withdrawal, a helicopter collided with a plane, killing eight men.

APRIL 30. Princess Beatrix became queen of the Netherlands when her mother, Queen Juliana, abdicated. Juliana had been queen for 32 years.

MAY 15. Maxie Anderson, 45, and his 23-year-old son, Kris, became the first people to balloon nonstop across North America. Their balloon, named the *Kitty Hawk,* took off from Fort Baker, California. Four days later it floated down on the Gaspé Peninsula of eastern Canada. In 1978, Maxie Anderson and two other men had become the first people to balloon across the Atlantic.

JUNE 27. President Carter signed a controversial draft registration bill. Under the bill, young men aged 19 and 20 must register with the Selective Service System. (Registration began on July 21. But there were no immediate plans for actually drafting the men into the armed services.)

JULY 11. Richard I. Queen, one of the American hostages held in Iran since November, 1979, was released so that he could receive medical treatment.

JULY 17. Zenko Suzuki was named premier of Japan by the parliament. He succeeded Masayoshi Ohira, who had died in June.

JULY 30. New Hebrides, a group of South Pacific islands, became the independent nation of Vanuatu. The islands had been ruled jointly by Britain and France for 74 years.

AUGUST 14. Some 17,000 Polish shipyard workers went on strike. The strike spread throughout much of Poland, causing a national crisis. (By the end of August, some 500,000 workers were on strike. They began returning to their jobs in early September, after being promised higher wages and important political gains. The workers won the right to form trade unions independent of the Communist Party. In no other Communist country is this possible. As a result of the strike, the country's leader, Edward Gierek, was forced to resign on September 6.)

AUGUST 20. The United States revealed that it had developed an "invisible" airplane—invisible, that is, to radar. The plane is called the stealth aircraft. It was built in a shape that has no sharp angles, because sharp angles are good reflectors of radar waves. The plane was also coated with a special material that helps to weaken radar waves.

SEPTEMBER 19. Terry Fox was awarded the Order of Canada, the highest medal a Canadian civilian can receive. The 22-year-old from British Columbia was the youngest person to receive the medal, which was awarded for his courage and perseverance. Fox had lost his right leg in 1977 because of bone cancer. After he was outfitted with an artificial leg, he began training to become a long-distance runner. On April 12, 1980, he began a 5,300-mile (8,350-kilometer) cross-Canada run, to raise money for medical research. He had completed more than half the distance before illness forced him to stop. His efforts raised millions of dollars for the Canadian Cancer Society.

SEPTEMBER 22. Iraqi airplanes bombed airfields in Iran. This marked the beginning of open warfare between the two Middle East countries.

OCTOBER 11. Two Soviet cosmonauts returned to Earth after setting a new record for time spent in space. Leonid Popov and Valery Ryumin spent 185 days aboard the Salyut 6 space station.

OCTOBER 23. Aleksei N. Kosygin resigned as premier of the Soviet Union. He had held that position for 16 years. He was succeeded by Nikolai A. Tikhonov.

NOVEMBER 4. In United States elections, Republicans Ronald W. Reagan and George H. Bush were elected president and vice-president. They defeated the Democratic candidates, incumbents Jimmy Carter and Walter F. Mondale.

DECEMBER 3. The *Solar Challenger*, an airplane powered by the rays of the sun, made a 22-minute flight over the Arizona desert. It was the longest solar flight on record. The *Solar Challenger* and an earlier test plane, the *Gossamer Penguin*, were the first to take off and fly using energy converted directly from the sun. The energy was gathered by solar cells on the wing and tail of the plane. The cells converted the solar energy to electricity, which ran the plane's motor.

13

WHOOOOO'S THAT HUNTER?

Darkness blankets the land. All is quiet. A hunter sits on a tree branch—watching, listening, waiting.

A mouse scurries along the ground. The patter of its tiny feet is heard by the hunter. In less than a second the hunter's eyes focus on the mouse. It swoops down, grabs the mouse with its sharp claws, and returns to the branch. It swallows the mouse whole.

The hunter is a barn owl. Within minutes of swallowing the mouse it is on the lookout for another victim. If the owl is fortunate, it will feed again and again during the night. It's a fact that one barn owl actually caught sixteen mice, three gophers, a rat, and a squirrel in only 25 minutes. He did not, however, eat all these animals himself. He shared them with his mate and their nestful of hungry youngsters.

The largest owl is the eagle owl (*above*), and the smallest is the least pygmy owl (*below*).

▶ MANY KINDS IN MANY PLACES

There are more than 130 kinds of owls. The smallest are the least pygmy owl of Central and South America and the elf owl of southern North America. They are about 5 inches (12 centimeters) long—about the size of a sparrow. The largest owl is the eagle owl that lives in Europe, Asia, and northern Africa. It may reach 30 inches (75 centimeters) in length.

Owls are found everywhere on the earth except Antarctica. They live in almost every kind of climate and habitat. Snowy owls prowl the snow-covered fields and tundra of the Arctic. Hawk owls, which have long tails and fly like falcons, inhabit woodlands. Elf

owls live in deserts. The Madagascar grass owl lives in tropical rain forests. Screech owls live in towns and cities.

▶ DISTINCTIVE FEATURES

Owls are easily recognized, for they share certain distinctive features. They have large heads and no obvious necks. Their eyes are large and are surrounded by feathers that radiate outward. The eyes are very sensitive, and owls can see in the dimmest light. In fact, some can see as well by starlight as people can see by moonlight.

An owl cannot move its eyes from side to side. If it wants to change its field of vision, it turns its head. Some types of owls can turn their heads more than 270 degrees to one side or the other. An owl can even turn its head upside down!

Owls are the only birds that blink like humans, by dropping their upper eyelids. (Other birds raise the lower lids.) When owls

Owls are found almost everywhere. Snowy owls live in the snow-covered Arctic . . .

sleep, however, they close their eyes by raising the lower lids.

The plumage of owls is very soft. Owls can puff up their feathers, and this helps keep them warm. It also makes them look bigger, which helps frighten enemies. Owls are never brightly colored. The plumage is a pattern of browns, grays, black, and white. This helps the owl blend into its surroundings so that it is nearly invisible to both prey and enemies. A snowy owl, which lives in snowy areas, is white or white and black. Owls that live in tropical rain forests are dark brown. Desert owls are generally pale and yellowish.

The owl's large, sensitive ears are hidden by feathers on the sides of its head. Some types of owls, like the long-eared owl and the great horned owl, have feathery "ears" or "horns" on their heads. These are not really ears or horns but simply tufts of long feathers that are a kind of decoration.

. . . and hawk owls inhabit woodlands.

The long-eared owl has feathery "ears" on the top of its head. They are not really ears but a kind of decoration.

An owl has short, powerful feet and very sharp claws. These are efficient weapons, both for catching prey and for fighting enemies. The outer toe can be moved forward, outward, and even backward. This makes it easier for the owl to grasp and hold a victim.

▶ A DIET OF MEAT

Owls are meat eaters. They do not eat plant matter. In general, rodents form the basis of their diets. But owls also eat other small mammals, reptiles, amphibians, insects, and earthworms. The oriental hawk owl is known to eat crabs. Some eagle owls dine almost exclusively on frogs. In Africa and Asia, there are species of owls that are fishers. They use their very sharp claws to scoop fish out of the water.

The larger the owl, the more it must eat and the larger the animals on which it can prey. The great hawk owls of Australia can tackle prey as large as rabbits and possums. Snowy owls eat primarily small rodents called lemmings. But they also eat larger animals such as hares and muskrats. They even catch ducks and other birds.

Most owls swallow small prey whole. Digestive juices secreted by the stomach break down the soft parts of the food. The parts that cannot be digested are regurgitated in neat little packages that are called pellets, or boluses.

By studying the contents of pellets, it is possible to learn about the diets of owls. Many interesting and important discoveries have been made in this manner. For example, giant barn owls once lived in the Caribbean. Their fossilized pellets are the only clue we have to the diet of these extinct birds.

Thanks to pellet analysis, the little owl of Europe was proved innocent of very serious charges. In the early 1900's, English farmers and gamekeepers accused the little owl of being a terrible poultry thief and a killer of game and song birds. Many English people wanted to kill the little owl, even though people in other parts of Europe were praising these birds for their ability to keep down rodent and insect populations.

An inquiry was made by a British scientific

A CLOSER LOOK AT OWL PELLETS

On the average, an owl forms two pellets each day. These can be found near the place where the owl roosts. If the owl changes its roosting spot often, its pellets will be scattered over a wide area. But if the owl always roosts in the same place, as barn owls do, then a pile of pellets will accumulate in one place.

If you find some owl pellets, try to identify the contents. First soak the pellets in warm water. When they are soft, use needles and tweezers to gently pull apart each pellet. Look at the contents of what you see.

Some of the things you will probably find are skulls, beaks, teeth, jaws, bones, fur, feathers, insect exoskeletons, and the tiny bristles from earthworm bodies. Mammal guidebooks are useful in identifying teeth. Bird guidebooks can be used to identify beaks and feathers from the pellets.

Most owls do not build their own nests. The tiny elf owl, for example, nests in holes in the giant saguaro cactus—holes made by other birds.

group. Nearly 2,500 food pellets from little owls were analyzed. Only two pellets contained the remains of young game birds. Only seven contained remains of poultry chicks. Most of the pellets contained the remains of rodent and insect pests. One pellet, for example, contained the remains of 343 earwigs! Since the results of the study were published, few English people have complained about the little owl.

▶ NESTS AND SONGS

Most owls do not build nests. Some use nests abandoned by eagles, crows, and other birds. Some lay their eggs in holes in trees. The tiny elf owl, for example, nests in holes in the giant saguaro cactus—holes made by woodpeckers and flickers.

The burrowing owl nests underground, usually in a prairie-dog community. It uses tunnels built by ground squirrels, armadillos, and other animals.

A female owl lays from one to twelve eggs. She sits on the eggs until they hatch. Meanwhile, her mate shares the food he catches with her. Depending on the species, it takes 27 to 36 days for the eggs to hatch. The baby birds, which are called nestlings or owlets, are born with their eyes and ears closed. The eyes and ears open when the birds are about a week old.

Owls generally do not live very long in the wild. A study of barn owls in Switzerland indicated that some reached the age of 9 years. But the average age of the barn owls was 16 months. In captivity, owls live longer. One tawny owl lived for 22 years in captivity, and an eagle owl reached the grand age of 68.

Not all owls call "whoo, whoo." The screech owl, the most common owl in North America, whistles. The barking owl of Australia can sound like a growling dog. Other owl calls include snores, coughs, and even pretty chirps.

An owl's calls serve the same functions as do the calls of other birds. Some calls are territorial: "This is my land, keep out." Other calls are made to attract mates. There are also calls that indicate fear, anger, and hunger. Most of the calls are not very loud. But some calls will carry over surprisingly great distances. The deep booming call of a snowy owl can be heard up to 7 miles (11 kilometers) away.

If you go for a walk tonight, watch and listen. Perhaps you will see or hear an owl. If you see one, stand quietly and watch it hunt. If you hear one, try to imitate its call. If you are successful, the owl may fly toward you, perch overhead, and call back to you.

JENNY TESAR
Series Consultant
Wonders of Wildlife

A

B

C

READ A ROAD SIGN

How fast can you read? Fast enough to understand a sign that says ROAD CLOSED TO ALL VEHICLES as you whiz past it in a car? What if the sign is in German—or Swahili?

Road signs of many countries solve this problem with pictures. Pictures can be understood instantly, by speakers of any language. And there are other clues. A sign's shape is one. In international signs, a triangle warns of danger, and a circle gives traffic rules. In North America, other shapes are used—a diamond, for instance, means danger. Color is also a clue. North American signs use red for stop and yellow for danger. Most drivers can easily "read" the pictures, shapes, and colors. Can you?

· 75 m ·

D

E

F

G

H

Look at these road signs. They come from all over the world. See if you can "read" what they are saying. Each sign has a letter under it. Match each one with its numbered meaning.

1. WATCH OUT FOR DEER, Virginia
2. WATCH OUT FOR BICYCLISTS, Denmark
3. WATCH OUT FOR TURTLES, Connecticut
4. WATCH OUT FOR CAMELS, Algeria
5. WATCH OUT FOR HIPPOS, Zambia
6. REFRESHMENTS NEARBY, Mexico
7. TRAIN CROSSING, France
8. GAS STATION NEARBY, California
9. WATCH OUT FOR ELEPHANTS, Zambia

ANSWERS:
A,3; B,7; C,2; D,8; E,1; F,5; G,6; H,9; I,4

I

Early on that Sunday morning, Mount St. Helens blew its top. It was a volcanic eruption with a force equal to 500 atomic bombs. Hot ash, gases, and rocks were hurled as high as 12 miles (19 kilometers) into the sky. The ash, rocks, and melting snow formed mudslides that clogged rivers. And a shockwave caused by the explosion leveled thousands of acres of Douglas fir trees—trees that had been the basis of the area's important lumber industry.

At least 34 people died as a result of the eruption. Another 28 were missing and presumed dead. The death toll of wildlife was almost impossible to imagine. Scientists believe that at least 1,500,000 game birds and mammals were killed. Nearly 11,000,000 fish died. And unknown millions of reptiles, amphibians, and insects also lost their lives.

The enormous mushroom-shaped cloud of particles thrown into the sky was carried eastward by air currents. It dropped huge amounts of ash and dust on the ground. This created major problems as far as 500 miles (800 kilometers) east of the volcano. The farmlands of eastern Washington were coated with the fine particles, and many crops were killed. In Idaho and Montana, the falling ash was so dense that days seemed to turn to dusk. In less than a week, the massive cloud of particles had passed over the eastern United States and Canada. It moved across the Atlantic and around the world. Fallout from the cloud will probably continue, at an ever decreasing rate, for years.

▶ **A VOLCANIC MOUNTAIN CHAIN**

Mount St. Helens is located in southwestern Washington, about 50 miles (80 kilometers) northeast of Portland, Oregon. It is part of the Cascades, a range of volcanic mountains that run from northern California into British Columbia. There are fifteen major volcanic mountains in the range. Among the best known are Lassen Peak, Mount Hood, Mount Rainier, Glacier Peak, and Mount Garibaldi. All these mountains have been active at some time during their lives. The last to erupt was Lassen Peak, in northern California. It erupted over a period of three years, from 1914 to 1917.

The last time Mount St. Helens erupted was in 1857. But scientists were expecting

MOUNT ST. HELENS AWAKENS

For 123 years, Mount St. Helens slept. It was a beautiful, peaceful sight. But in March, 1980, the mountain began to awaken. Earthquakes were the first signs of life. Then for more than six weeks the mountain hurled steam and ash into the sky.

Still, few people were prepared for the events of May 18.

another eruption. In 1975 the United States Geological Survey said that Mount St. Helens was the Cascade volcano most likely to reawaken from dormancy (sleep), "perhaps before the end of this century."

The May 18 eruption was just the first of many for Mount St. Helens. A May 25 eruption dumped ash on cities in coastal Oregon and Washington. Portland International Airport had to be closed temporarily, and telephone and electric transmission lines failed. In June, July, August, and October it erupted again. How many more times it will erupt is unknown. It may return to a dormant state, or it may continue to spew material into the air for years and years.

▶ SOME GAINS FROM THE DESTRUCTION

Scientists immediately showed a great interest in Mount St. Helens' activity. They conducted research at the mountain in the hope of learning what causes volcanoes to explode. They also searched for signs that would indicate an eruption was about to occur. Such signs would enable scientists to predict eruptions.

Other scientists tried to determine the long-term effects of Mount St. Helens' eruptions on people and their activities. The ash and other material expelled by the eruptions were not expected to affect human health. Whether they would affect the weather was debated. Some scientists believed that the particles remaining in the atmosphere would have a slight cooling effect on the earth's temperature.

The ash that fell on farmlands may improve the soil because it contains minerals needed for plant growth. As a matter of fact, volcanic regions often make good farmlands for this reason.

Some of the millions of trees laying like matchsticks on the mountain's slopes were salvaged. They will provide lumber for housing and other construction. When all the logs are removed, the area can be reseeded.

But it will be years before forests again cover the slopes of Mount St. Helens—assuming of course, that the slopes will remain. Whole sections of the mountaintop have been blown away. It's possible that future eruptions will destroy even more of the mountain. Perhaps Mount St. Helens will disappear, as did another volcanic mountain in the Cascades. About 6,600 years ago, a mountain called Mazama exploded. It no longer exists. Its location is marked by a beautiful lake named, appropriately enough, Crater Lake. Will Mount St. Helens suffer the same fate as Mazama?

Below: The particles thrown into the sky from the volcano dropped huge amounts of ash on the ground. Right: The explosion also leveled thousands of fir trees —the basis of the area's important lumber industry.

HAPPY BIRTHDAY, DISNEYLAND

The year 1980 marked 25 years of dreams-come-true for Disneyland—"the happiest place on earth." The celebrations held during the Magic Kingdom's 25th year made up one of the longest, biggest, and brightest birthday parties ever seen.

When Disneyland opened on July 17, 1955, in Anaheim, California, guests quickly recognized that it was like no other place on earth. Through the years, Walt Disney's Magic Kingdom has become a symbol of happiness to the world. Nearly 200,000,000 people of all ages, including kings, queens, and presidents, have shared in the special magic and fun that is Disneyland.

The Magic Kingdom was a twenty-year dream-come-true for Walt Disney. Walt was known as both the "showman of the world" and Disneyland's chief "imagineer." He was also the "father" of such lovable characters as Mickey Mouse, Donald Duck, and Goofy.

Walt began to dream about his new idea in family entertainment during the 1930's. "Disneyland really began," Walt said, "when my two daughters were very young. Saturday was always 'Daddy's Day,' and I would take them to a merry-go-round, and

sit on a bench eating peanuts while they rode. And sitting there, alone, I felt that there should be something built, some kind of a family park where parents and children could have fun together."

The place Walt dreamed of, and began planning to create, was not to be just another amusement park. It was to be something both marvelous and unique. "I don't want the public to see the world they live in while they are in Disneyland," Walt said. "I want them to feel they are in another world." And that is just what he achieved.

▶ **THE SEVEN LANDS**

Disneyland is an entertainment world made up of seven "lands." Each land is a realm of yesterday or tomorrow, fantasy or adventure. (1) **Main Street, U.S.A.,** recaptures the friendly way of life in smalltown America at the turn of the century. (2) In **Fantasyland,** storybook dreams and Disney film classics come to life for both the young and young at heart. (3) **Adventureland** is a wonderland of nature's own design, where adventure lurks around every bend. (4) In **Frontierland,** the pioneer backwoods of

Davy Crockett, Mark Twain's riverboat country, and the Wild West can be explored. Highlighting the many Frontierland adventures is Big Thunder Mountain Railroad, which you can board for a headlong race through an avalanche. (5) The future is now in **Tomorrowland,** where the stout-hearted can be launched on a twisting, turning rocket journey through Space Mountain. (6) **New Orleans Square** is the home of the rowdy Pirates of the Caribbean, and also of the 999 happy ghosts, ghouls, and goblins who are just "dying" to meet you in the Haunted Mansion. (7) **Bear Country,** Disneyland's newest land, is the setting for the rip-roaring-est show in the woods—the Country Bear Jamboree. This foot-stompin', hillbilly hoedown features a zany den of singin' and fiddle-playin' bears.

Walt Disney, the creator of Disneyland.

▶ THE BIRTHDAY CELEBRATION

Disneyland's 25th birthday party was a spectacular, year-long celebration, featuring a special parade presented daily. Led by Mickey Mouse and the Disneyland Band, the colorful pageant saluted each of the seven lands with fanfare, music, and fun. From Main Street, U.S.A.'s comical Keystone Kops and the Royal Street Bachelors of New Orleans Square—to Adventureland's Tahitian Terrace Dancers and Cinderella's Crystal Coach from Fantasyland—the parade was memory-filled with Disney delights.

The year 1980 was a time to celebrate some of the many special moments that helped make Disneyland "the happiest place on earth" during its first 25 years. But any day is a special day in Disneyland, perfect for enjoying its world of adventure and fantasy, yesterday and tomorrow.

One of the most beautiful highlights of the birthday parade was Cinderella's Crystal Coach.

The Enchanted Figs

Once upon a time, in the sunny Spanish kingdom of Valencia, there lived a widowed queen and her son and daughter, Prince Victor and Princess Victoria.

Queen Maria's northern border was in constant danger of invasion by her neighbor, the wicked King Carlos of Catalonia. Unfortunately, the Queen was not a rich monarch, and she certainly didn't have enough gold in her treasury to support a large army. So she provided for the safety of her kingdom in a unique fashion.

Queen Maria used what little gold she did have to hire a wandering wizard instead of an army. The wizard planted a ring of fig trees around the kingdom and put a spell on them, so that anyone who looked at one of the enchanted trees would be unable to resist eating a fig. And anyone who ate an enchanted fig would be turned into a sheep.

The Queen also made provision for friends and merchants to visit Valencia. She selected a narrow pass and instructed the wizard not to plant any fig trees there. A small force could easily defend the pass against any hostile army.

After the Queen had paid the wizard for his services, he gave her a parting gift: a magic talisman. It was a moonstone, which hung from a heavy gold chain around her neck. The wizard showed her how to hold up the jewel in front of her, and taught her two rhymes. The first would render the spell of the magic figs harmless; the second would reverse it. The secret of the rhymes was known only to the royal family and to the royal chamberlain, Don Pedro.

Looking forward to peace at last, Queen Maria sent a warning to King Carlos, advising him to leave her in peace. But King Carlos, with the natural arrogance of a bully, thought she was bluffing. He equipped his army and sent it against the kingdom of Valencia. His line of attack led right through the ring of enchanted fig trees, with the results you might expect: King Carlos lost an army, and Queen Maria gained a flock of sheep.

And since King Carlos' army had been a large one, Queen Maria's flock was also large. She soon had a thriving wool business and enough revenue to fill her treasury to bursting.

The Queen was now so wealthy, in fact, that her chamberlain, Don Pedro, became jealous of her fortune and began to hatch a plot to take over her kingdom.

"I must be careful not to get the people too stirred up by moving too quickly,"

Pedro plotted. "I'll get rid of those two brats first. Then I'll get the Queen out of the way, and *I'll* be king of Valencia. Ha, ha, ha!"

Pleased with his plot, Pedro paced the palace until he was sure everyone was asleep. Then he sneaked into the Queen's chamber and stole her magic moonstone. He crept along the corridor to the Prince's bedroom, knocked the boy unconscious, and carried him down to the courtyard.

The wicked chamberlain bound Prince Victor hand and foot and returned to the castle for the Princess. He knocked her out, tied her up, and deposited her next to her brother in a cart.

Don Pedro drove the cart straight for the enchanted fig grove. When he drew up under one of the trees, he held up the Queen's moonstone and recited the spell:

"Magic fig, your spell deny—
Let me pass you safely by!"

The crafty chamberlain threw the Prince and Princess on the ground and left them to their fate.

As he turned back toward the castle, he laughed evilly. "There, royal brats," he gloated. "Soon you will be only two more sheep in *my* flock." During the ride back, he planned how he would deal with the Queen as soon as the uproar over the disappearance of the Prince and Princess had died down.

As luck would have it, Prince Victor began to regain consciousness in time to hear Don Pedro's boast. As soon as he heard the word "sheep," he knew what the chamberlain was planning, and he was careful to keep his eyes tightly shut as he squirmed out of his bonds.

The Prince groped toward his sister. His hands discovered her satin robe. But when he felt further, his fingers found only woolly fluff. When he touched it, it let out a plaintive "baaa!"

Poor Prince Victor! He knew immediately that his sister had also awakened. And with no warning, she had looked upon the enchanted trees. She had eaten a fig and been turned into a lamb.

"Oh, Sister," groaned the Prince, "why couldn't you have slept a little longer?"

But all the lamb could answer was, "baaa!"

"Well," said the Prince, his eyes still closed, "then you must lead us through the grove to Aragon. Surely King Alfonso will help us."

"Baaa," answered the lamb, which the Prince took to mean "yes."

The next morning a bedraggled Prince and a little gray lamb presented themselves to King Alfonso and requested an audience.

"Well, hello there, boy," hailed the King. "My, what a cute little pet you have—although I would have expected that a fellow your age would have a dog. But what brings you to visit me?"

When Prince Victor explained what had happened, King Alfonso grew serious. "I never did trust that chamberlain," he said, "and now I know I was right. You may be sure he has told your mother some tall tale about how you've run away or been kidnapped. And with you out of the way, she'll be at his mercy.

"Now, I'd lend you my army to march on the castle and take him prisoner, except that he can easily defend that narrow pass. And we can't just cross the border, because of those dratted fig trees your mother planted. I told her she'd be sorry if she did that, but she refused to listen to me."

"I do agree, Sire," began the Prince respectfully. "Your army wouldn't do me any good, but I do need your help. Would you send for your secretary?"

"Of course, my boy," replied the King, "but I don't see how that will help."

When the secretary arrived with his parchment and quills, the Prince dictated a letter. " '. . . the boy seems highly confused, Your Majesty,' " he concluded, " 'and he has a pet lamb with him that he keeps calling Victoria. Please Madame, you must advise me. Yours, etc.'

"Now, King Alfonso, if you will sign this, we can send it by messenger to Valencia."

"Of course, my boy," said the King, "but your mother will never receive it. The chamberlain is sure to intercept it."

"That's what I'm hoping," explained Prince Victor. "As soon as Don Pedro reads this, he'll rush here to finish what he started. But we'll be ready for him," said the Prince confidently.

The following day, Don Pedro arrived at the castle.

"Oh, Don Pedro," cried King Alfonso when the chamberlain was brought into his presence. "I hope you've come to tell me what to do about poor Prince Victor."

"Yes, Sire, Queen Maria sent me," replied Pedro craftily. "She received your letter, and she sent me to bring her son back."

"He has been saying some pretty strange things," the King said, hesitating.

"He raves, Sire," explained Don Pedro. "The boy took a nasty fall from his pony yesterday, and he's not in his right mind."

"I guess it must be as you say," answered the King. "I'll send for the child. Meanwhile, why don't you have some of this excellent Madeira wine?"

"Thank you, Sire," replied Don Pedro, sure that he had fooled the King.

King Alfonso filled a goblet and brought it

to the chamberlain. But as he was approaching Don Pedro, he tripped. Grabbing for something to steady himself, King Alfonso's fingers fastened on the heavy gold chain around the chamberlain's neck. It wasn't enough to break his fall, and King and pendant crashed to the floor.

"How clumsy of me," apologized the King. "I'll have this repaired right away." And he commanded a page to take the pendant to the royal goldsmith.

Of course Don Pedro protested, saying he could get it fixed back at his own castle, but King Alfonso was firm. "Tut, tut, my dear man," he soothed. "I'll have it fixed right here, in a jiffy."

Sure enough, in a few minutes the page returned with Don Pedro's pendant, as good as new.

A servant appeared with the Prince and his little pet lamb. Don Pedro began to hustle the boy away. "Well, thank you, King Alfonso. We'd better be going now—can't keep the Queen waiting."

As soon as they were out of the castle, Don Pedro hoisted the Prince, none too gently, into a cart. He whipped up the horse

and off they galloped. The little lamb trailed behind, trying to keep up.

They soon reached the grove of enchanted fig trees, and Don Pedro confidently raised the pendant and recited the magic rhyme. Then slowly he began to get down from the cart. "That's funny," he said to himself. "I'm really hungry for one of those figs."

Hastily the wicked chamberlain again held up the moonstone and recited the rhyme. But still he kept walking toward the tree, as if drawn by an invisible cord.

Then Don Pedro realized what must have happened. "Oh, no!" he cried.

Prince Victor watched with satisfaction as the evil chamberlain ran to the tree, plucked a fig, and gobbled it greedily. Don Pedro met the same fate he had so cruelly planned for the Prince and Princess.

"So much for that plot," said the Prince, taking an identical moonstone necklace from his pocket and reciting the magic spell. This time it worked, for King Alfonso had cleverly had his goldsmith switch a copy of the magic talisman for the real one.

Just then a little gray lamb trotted up, all out of breath. "Oh, there you are, Victoria," the Prince called. "Come here!"

Prince Victor again raised the magical moonstone and recited the rhyme that would free Victoria from the fig tree's spell:

"Fig of power, I've found the knack—
Reverse your spell and turn her back!"

Then the Prince and Princess climbed up on the cart and set off for their castle, where they were reunited with their mother and lived happily ever after.

THE PEARLIES OF LONDON

For most people in London, life is similar to that in any big city. They work or go to school, take care of their homes, and try to get a little rest and relaxation on weekends and holidays. But for one small group of Londoners, weekends and holidays are different. As if touched by a fairy godmother's magic wand, they are transformed into royalty, in clothes that glitter and glow with the sheen of thousands of pearls.

These people are the Pearlies—proud bearers of a tradition that is nearly 100 years old. Their name comes from their costumes, which are covered with mother-of-pearl buttons. And their story begins in the late 1800's, with fruit-and-vegetable venders called costermongers. (A coster is a kind of apple; "monger" means "salesperson.")

The costermongers sold their wares on the streets of London. They were flashy dressers because eye-catching clothes—especially those with a few bright buttons—helped attract attention to their stands. Street selling wasn't an easy way to make a living, and the costermongers were poor. Still, they tried to help people who were needier than they were. They would often dress up and hold parades to raise money for local hospitals and other charities.

A young man named Henry Croft took part in one of these parades. Henry had grown up in an orphanage, where he had been taught how to sew, and he decided to make a very unusual costume for the parade. He sewed mother-of-pearl buttons all over his clothes.

The costermongers loved Henry's outfit. And Henry became known as the Pearly King. Soon, some of the costermongers were copying Henry's idea. They, too, decorated their clothes with closely sewn buttons.

Henry decided that every district of London should be a Pearly Kingdom and have a Pearly King and Queen. The first kings and queens were elected, and their titles became hereditary—that is, the titles were passed on

to their children. Only when a king and queen had no children was a new royal couple elected.

At one time, there were hundreds of Pearlies in London. But their number has decreased sharply. After World War II, many Pearly families moved out of London to the suburbs. And lifestyles changed. The costermonger stalls were replaced by supermarkets. Mother-of-pearl buttons that once were plentiful and cheap became hard to find and expensive. And younger members of some Pearly families weren't interested in keeping up the tradition. Today there are fewer than 35 Pearlies left.

The Pearlies who remain are members of a Pearly Guild and work hard to uphold their traditions. They put on their glittering costumes for dances, fashion shows, garden parties, and other charitable events in London. The children of the king and queen often take part in these activities. They have costumes, too, and they are called princes and princesses. Even pet dogs sometimes get into the act, wearing pearly collars and cloths as they trot beside the royal family.

Usually each person makes his or her own costume. Suits, dresses, shirts—even ties and hats—are covered with mother-of-pearl buttons. It takes at least 20,000 buttons to decorate a man's suit. One Pearly Queen's dress is covered with 30,000 buttons, and her coat with 60,000 buttons. As you can imagine, it takes months to sew all the buttons on the clothes. And the finished costumes can be very heavy. Some outfits weigh as much as 70 pounds (30 kilograms).

The buttons are sewn on to form flowers, boats, bells, hearts, and other complicated patterns. Each Pearly family has its own design. The Morris family design includes a pattern of doves. The Arrowsmith family is recognized by the butterflies that decorate its costumes. And on the back of each outfit is the name of the Pearly's "kingdom"— an area of London such as Whitechapel, Hampstead, or Lambeth.

As in years gone by, Pearlies don't get paid for their appearances. The money they raise goes to charity. Over the decades the Pearlies have raised many thousands of dollars for sick, needy, and disabled people.

ANIMALS IN DANGER

Pandas, sea turtles, condors, manatees—four very different kinds of animals. But they share a common problem. All of them are threatened with extinction. Their populations are getting smaller and smaller. Unless something is done to help these animals, they may soon cease to exist.

The animals' problems have been caused mainly by people. People have destroyed the forests where pandas lived. They have killed condors for their feathers, sea turtles for their meat and shells, and manatees for their meat, blubber, and hides. Poisons put out to kill predators have instead been eaten by condors. Motorboat propellers have injured and killed manatees. Shrimping nets have caught sea turtles, causing them to drown.

Biologists and other people are trying to save these four animals. It is too soon to know if their efforts will be successful. It would be a tragedy if even one of the four became extinct. Here is what the world would lose:

▶ **THE GIANT PANDA**

Everyone knows the giant panda. This black and white creature is one of the world's most loved animals. It looks like a bear, but it is believed to be more closely related to the raccoon family. Of course, it is much bigger than a raccoon. A full-grown giant panda can weigh up to 300 pounds (135 kilograms). When it stretches up on its hind legs it reaches a height of about 5 feet (1.5 meters).

The giant panda is a shy animal. It lives alone except during the mating season. Its home is in China, in dense mountain forests. Its main food is bamboo. It may eat 20 pounds (9 kilograms) of bamboo a day. It also eats fruits, berries, bulbs, and even small animals.

The panda is a night creature. During the day it sleeps in a tree hollow or on a shady branch. It uses its tail as a pillow—or to cover its face.

A panda is very tiny at birth. It weighs only about 5 ounces (140 grams) and looks like a hairless mouse. It spends much of its time eating, and within ten weeks weighs 25 to 30 times as much.

Mother pandas take very good care of their babies. When the baby is 2 months old, the mother begins to play with it—tossing it

These pandas are dining on bamboo, the most important food of their diet. Many pandas have starved to death because some species of bamboo are scarce.

from one arm to another, tickling it, perhaps playing a game of peekaboo. If the baby is unhappy, she will caress it with her paw, much as a human mother caresses her baby.

The giant panda is the national symbol of China. No one knows how many giant pandas exist, but scientists believe there are fewer than 1,000. Recently, China established a special nature preserve in the western part of the country to protect the pandas that live there. The Chinese have also had some success in breeding pandas in zoos. In 1980, a panda was born in a zoo in Mexico City—the first born in captivity outside China. But it lived barely more than a week. Zookeepers are hopeful that in the next few years they will have greater success in breeding pandas.

▶ SEA TURTLES

When Spanish explorers first traveled to the Americas, they had a unique way of navigating through the fog off Grand Cayman Island. They would follow the sounds made by huge herds of sea turtles.

There are seven species of sea turtles. Six of them are endangered. The Atlantic ridley is closest to extinction. As recently as 40 years ago, they were still plentiful. People could watch 40,000 ridleys nesting on a beach in Mexico. Today, there are probably only 500 to 1,000 nesting females left on earth.

Sea turtles are big. Some weigh 500 pounds (225 kilograms) or more. Unlike land turtles, a sea turtle cannot pull its head or legs into its shell. The front legs are broad and flat. They are used to propel the animal through the water. The back legs are short and serve as rudders for steering.

International efforts to protect sea turtles are under way. Many countries have passed laws that make it illegal to capture turtles. But these laws are hard to enforce. One reason for the difficulty is that many sea turtles travel great distances. When it is time to nest, sea turtles return to the beach where they were born. How they find the beach is still a mystery to scientists. So is the reason for the migration. Why do they travel as much as 2,000 miles (3,200 kilometers) to reach the beach where they were born when other beaches—used by other turtles of the same species—are nearer?

Generally, the males stay in the shallow coastal waters while the females go onto the beach. The females go to sand dunes high on the beach, well above the high tide mark. They dig holes in the sand, lay their eggs, and then cover the eggs with sand.

A sea turtle's broad front legs are used to propel the animal through water. Sea turtles have been hunted for their meat and shells.

The California condor is the largest bird in North America. Only 30 of these birds remain on earth.

When the young turtles hatch, they immediately head for the water. This is the most dangerous moment in their lives. Many are caught and eaten by predators such as gulls and wild dogs before they can reach the water.

Scientists are experimenting with raising baby turtles in laboratories. The turtles are kept in the lab until they are a year old. Then, when they are old enough to fend for themselves, they are released into the sea.

Some people are trying to raise sea turtles on "farms." Not everyone agrees with this. Supporters say farming is a way to save sea turtles and at the same time meet people's demands for turtle soup and turtle steaks. Critics say farming will only increase the demand for turtle products, thereby increasing the illegal hunting of these scarce animals.

▶ THE CALIFORNIA CONDOR

The California condor is the biggest bird in North America. Large specimens weigh about 30 pounds (14 kilograms) and have wingspans of about 9 feet (3 meters).

On the ground the condor seems awkward. But few birds are as beautiful in the air. Once it is high in the sky, it moves on rising currents of warm air. It can soar for an hour or longer without once flapping its wings. If it spots food, it will quickly return to earth. The condor is a scavenger. It eats only the flesh of dead animals—mainly cattle, sheep, and deer but also small mammals such as rodents and rabbits.

The condor lives in rocky, mountainous areas around the southern end of California's San Joaquin Valley. It roosts in a tree or on a cliff. Its favorite roost is a tall dead conifer. These trees have no leaves to block the condor's view or to obstruct its flight. And such trees do not sway much in the wind. This is important because the condor's toes cannot grasp strongly.

The bird likes to sun itself in the early morning. It extends its wings to the sides to catch the sun. Every so often it turns around, to sun its other side. After a day of sunning, soaring, and eating, the bird tucks its head under the feathers on its back and goes to sleep.

At one time, condors could be found throughout California and in Oregon, Nevada, Utah, and Arizona. But as people cultivated more land and turned ranchlands into housing developments, the large grazing animals on which condors feed became scarce. People also shot many condors. And in recent years the birds have been killed by eating poisoned meat meant for coyotes. Only about 30 California condors remain on earth. Even optimists place their chance of survival at no more than 50–50.

▶ MANATEES

When Christopher Columbus sailed to the New World, he wrote in his log: "I saw three mermaids, but they were not as beautiful as they were painted." What Columbus actually saw were manatees—large gray mammals with whiskers and wrinkled skin. Not very beautiful, perhaps. But manatees are among the gentlest and most trusting animals on earth.

There are three species of manatees. One is found in the coastal waters of the Caribbean. The second lives in the Amazon basin. And the third species lives in the rivers of western Africa.

Manatees are plant eaters. They feed on water hyacinths and other water plants. A manatee eats at least 60 pounds (27 kilograms) of food a day. When eating, manatees use their flippers much as you use your hands, to guide the plants to their mouths. Their huge appetites can be very helpful to people—manatees can be used to keep waterways free of weeds.

When not eating, manatees like to rest just beneath the water's surface. Every few minutes they will stick their nostrils above the water's surface to breathe.

Adult manatees can weigh up to 1,200 pounds (550 kilograms). Like whales, they have been hunted for their meat, blubber, and hides. Many have been killed by sport hunters, and some countries have now set up special manatee refuges.

No one knows how many manatees are alive today. About 1,000 are thought to live in Florida, where there are a number of refuges. Boaters are warned to reduce their speed in these areas, so that they can see and avoid hitting the manatees. And there are fines and jail sentences for people who bother these gentle creatures.

Manatees are among the gentlest of animals. They have been injured and killed by motorboat propellers.

HANDS-ON ART

This art exhibit turned the tables on museum visitors and made them part of the show. The exhibit, at the San Francisco Museum of Modern Art in 1980, was called Project Hands-On. It featured a group of paintings done on metal, by California artist Jananne Lassetter—all of them incomplete.

Hanging on the walls were realistic landscapes, abstracts of colored stripes or squares, and plain white canvases. Nearby were magnetized cutouts of everything from insects to hot-air balloons, as well as colorful geometric shapes. Visitors were invited to step up and finish the paintings by sticking on the cutouts. A striped abstract might become a seascape or a desert scene. A landscape might be peopled with geometric forms or animals. Or a visitor might just have fun experimenting with the cutout shapes on a white canvas.

Lassetter's idea was to let people learn firsthand how artists use shape, color, space, and scale to create pictures. And she liked what the visitors did. "Maybe I've found a quick way to discover genius," she said.

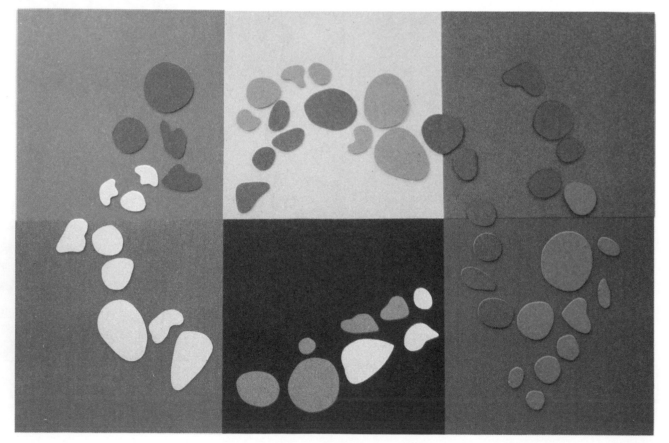

BLOWING IN THE WIND

A wind from the west
Brings weather at its best;
A wind from the east
Brings rain to man and beast.

Will the weather be fair or foul? To learn the latest forecast, you can simply pick up a newspaper or switch on the radio or TV. But 100 years ago, farmers, sailors—in fact, anyone who wanted or needed to know what the next day's weather might be—had to make their own forecasts.

Since ancient times, one of the tools people have used to predict weather has been the weather vane—the familiar rooftop device that shows the direction of the wind. Knowing which way the wind is blowing is helpful in forecasting because certain kinds of weather tend to come along with winds from certain directions. But over the centuries, weather vanes have taken on other uses as well. They have become symbols of power and religion, signs for merchants and tradespeople, and a unique form of folk art.

▶ THE VANES OF THE OLD WORLD

No one knows who made the first weather vane. But one of the most famous vanes of the ancient world was built in Athens, during the 1st century B.C., by the Greek astronomer Andronicus. Andronicus mounted his vane on an eight-sided structure called the Tower of the Winds. The vane itself was a figure of Triton (the half-man, half-fish god of the sea) carrying a wand in one hand. When the wind blew, the figure swung around so that the wand pointed in the direction from which the wind was coming. The Triton vane set the pattern for later vanes in two important ways—it pointed into the wind, and it was decorative as well as useful.

Like the Greeks, the Romans used weather vanes. And through their empire, vanes spread across Europe. Two designs that are still used on weather vanes today—the banner and the cock—developed in Europe during the Middle Ages. Nobles, who by law were the only people allowed to fly banners and pennants, adopted the banner design. Banner vanes showing heraldic de-

The cock is a weather-vane design that developed in Europe during the Middle Ages. It is still popular today.

vices were placed on castle turrets to advertise the owner's rank.

Weather vanes in the form of cocks (roosters), on the other hand, were connected with religion. In the 9th century, the Roman Catholic Church ordered that every church be topped with the figure of a cock, a symbol associated with Saint Peter. Medieval artisans combined the cocks with weather vanes. This design became so widespread that its name, the weathercock, was often used to refer to any weather vane.

Gradually cocks, banners, simple arrows, and more elaborate designs began to be seen on the shops of merchants and homes of common people, as well as on churches and castles. But as a form of folk art, the weather vane reached its peak in North America—especially in the United States—during the 18th and 19th centuries.

▶ THE VANES OF AMERICA

In America, blacksmiths and woodcarvers turned out finely crafted vanes with devices that ranged from cows and horses to mermaids and square-rigger ships. Many of the early vanes were one-of-a-kind designs. A gilded copper grasshopper, for example, was placed on Boston's Faneuil Hall in 1742. It was made by Shem Drowne, who is thought to have been the first American artisan to make a living by designing and building weather vanes.

Other early designs were only slightly less fanciful. Paul Revere topped his coppersmith shop with a wooden codfish. George Washington favored a dove, carrying an olive branch as a sign of peace, for his estate, Mount Vernon. Seafaring designs were seen in coastal towns. Vanes sporting cows, hogs, and sheep were placed on barns that housed these animals. And figures of American Indians were especially popular in western Pennsylvania and New York—perhaps to show that the settlers wanted to be on friendly terms with Indian tribes.

During the 19th century, when patriotic feeling was strong in the United States, eagles and figures of Columbia, the goddess of liberty, topped town halls everywhere. Another popular subject for 19th-century vanes was the horse, which was essential for work and transportation. Vanes patterned after

An unusual weather vane is this copper grasshopper, which has topped Boston's Faneuil Hall since 1742.

Seafaring designs such as mermaids and fish were often seen in coastal towns.

Figures of American Indians were especially popular in Pennsylvania and New York.

workhorses, riding horses, and famous trotting horses raced the wind from the roofs of homes and barns.

In the 19th century, too, vanes became trade signs. A mortar-and-pestle vane might be seen over an apothecary shop, where medicines were made and sold. A figure of a locomotive might mark a railroad station, and a fire-engine vane might swing in the breeze over a firehouse.

The artisans who made these vanes were often traveling carpenters and blacksmiths. They sold their handiwork door-to-door or at taverns along the road. Most of the vanes were flat, carved from wood or shaped from iron or sheet metal. But some were hollow, three-dimensional figures, made by hammering thin sheets of copper into molds for the various parts of the figure. The shaped cop-

A figure of a locomotive marked a train station.

The horse was a popular design because it was important for work and transportation.

per pieces were then soldered together. Gold leaf or paint was often used to finish the figure.

By the 20th century, factory methods were being used to make most weather vanes. These mass-produced vanes often lacked the originality and fine design of the earlier ones. Vanes remained popular, however. Today a few artisans still make them by hand. And scientists who study weather still use vanes, often in combination with devices that measure and record wind speed.

Some of the old, handcrafted weather vanes can still be seen atop homes, churches, and town halls. But still another use has been found for these vanes—they have become popular collector's items. Today many of the finest ones can be seen in museums of folk art.

On January 20, 1981, Ronald Reagan was to be inaugurated the 40th president of the United States.

THE U.S. PRESIDENTIAL ELECTION

In the 1980 presidential election, the people of the United States voted for change. By a solid margin, they chose Ronald Reagan, a Republican, over Democratic President Jimmy Carter. Reagan, a former movie star and ex-governor of California, had sought the presidency twice before. At 69, he was the oldest person ever elected to the office. And when he and his running mate, George Bush, defeated Carter and Vice-President Walter Mondale, the longest presidential campaign in U.S. history came to an end.

Reagan and Carter had received their parties' nominations only after long struggles against other contenders. The race started in August, 1978, when Republican Philip Crane announced that he was running for president. Other Republicans began tossing their hats into the ring, too—Reagan; Bush, a former congressman from Texas and, later, U.S. delegate to the United Nations; Howard Baker, senator from Tennessee; Robert Dole, senator from Kansas; John Connally, former governor of Texas; John Anderson, congressman from Illinois.

In other years, a president in office could often be assured of being automatically renominated by his party. But in 1980, two prominent Democrats rose to challenge Carter for the nomination—Jerry Brown, governor of California, and Ted Kennedy, senator from Massachusetts.

▶ PRIMARIES AND CAUCUSES

Between February and June, 1980, 37 states held primary elections. A primary gives people a chance to vote for the candidate they think their party should nominate. Delegates representing the primary winners go to the national party convention, where the candidate is actually chosen. In the states that did not have primaries, the parties held caucuses (meetings) in each of their districts. At these meetings, local party members voted for candidates or delegates.

Gradually, some of the presidential hopefuls withdrew because they did not have enough support. In the Republican race, the choice narrowed down to Reagan, Bush, and Anderson. By May, Reagan had enough delegates to win the nomination, and Bush abandoned his campaign.

Anderson hadn't won any primaries. But a good many Democrats, as well as liberal Republicans, supported him. He decided to run as an independent. He was the most important candidate to challenge the two big parties. Other candidates, such as Barry Commoner of the Citizens' Party and Ed Clark of the Libertarian Party, were not expected to draw many votes.

The Democratic fight was affected when, late in 1979, Iranians seized the U.S. embassy in Teheran and held some 50 Americans there hostage. Carter said the crisis would prevent him from traveling around the country, and he limited his campaign efforts to press conferences. Kennedy charged that Carter was using the crisis to avoid discussing important issues.

In April, the United States made an unsuccessful attempt to rescue the hostages. After that, Carter began to campaign more actively. In primaries and caucuses, he won 60 percent of the delegates to the Democratic convention. Brown withdrew. But Kennedy said that people who had voted for Carter in the early primaries no longer favored him. Kennedy wanted to change a convention rule that required delegates to vote for their candidates. Carter said that if the rules were changed, people who had voted for him in the primaries would be cheated.

The Republicans held their convention in Detroit from July 14 to 17. They adopted a conservative platform. (A platform is a statement of the party's positions on various issues.) Then they overwhelmingly endorsed Reagan as their candidate. In his acceptance speech, Reagan called for a renewal of the American spirit.

Even before the convention began, the biggest question had been who would be Reagan's running mate. Many Republicans felt that former president Gerald Ford would be the best choice. But Reagan and Ford failed to agree on the amount of authority that Ford would have as vice-president. And so, at the last moment, Reagan turned to the person who had been his most serious challenger for the presidential nomination—George Bush.

The Democratic National Convention was held in New York City from August 11 to 14. Early on the first day, Kennedy lost his fight to change the convention rules, and he withdrew from the race. But several of his programs became part of the party platform at the convention.

Carter, in accepting his party's nomination, said: "This election is a stark choice between . . . two sharply different pictures of what America is and what the world is. But it's more than that. It's a choice between two futures."

▶ A CLEAR CHOICE

The presidential candidates and their parties had significantly different positions on a number of important issues.

The Economy. Reagan called for a large income tax cut—30 percent over three years. He also said that the federal budget could be greatly cut and could be balanced by 1983. He favored the growth of private business to create jobs and improve the economy.

Carter favored a relatively small tax cut, saying a large cut would add to inflation. He said the budget couldn't be balanced (a promise he had made during his 1976 campaign) without losing important programs. The Democratic platform proposed government action to create jobs.

Energy. Reagan emphasized energy production. He said that the energy crisis had been caused primarily by federal regulations that discouraged production of oil and gas in the United States. He placed more stress on ending such controls than on conserving energy resources.

Carter stressed conservation. He felt that the government should play a major role in financing the development of synthetic fuels and other new energy sources.

Environment. Reagan said that many environmental regulations were unnecessary and had resulted in the loss of jobs. He favored

John Anderson, who ran as an independent, was the most important candidate to challenge both major parties.

President Jimmy Carter and Reagan greet each other before their October 28 debate.

giving states control over large tracts of undeveloped land now owned by the federal government.

Carter supported existing laws that protect the environment. He said he would not sacrifice environmental protection for industry. He favored legislation that would protect federal wilderness lands in Alaska.

Foreign Policy. The Republicans called for a strong stand against the spread of Communism. Reagan said that the United States should have a "hands-off" attitude toward the domestic policies, including human rights policies, of friendly countries. And he was cautious about developing closer ties with China.

Carter had established full diplomatic relations with China, and his concern about human rights had influenced U.S. policy toward other countries. The Democratic platform condemned aggressive Soviet acts but called for the easing of tensions between East and West.

Defense and Military Issues. Reagan said he would scrap the SALT II arms control treaty and negotiate a new agreement. He said the United States must maintain military superi-

ority, and he called for a buildup of military equipment. Reagan opposed registration for the draft.

Carter supported SALT II. He had ordered registration of 19- and 20-year-olds for the draft, but he said he was against a peacetime draft. He also called for increased military spending.

Social Issues. Reagan opposed the Equal Rights Amendment (ERA), although he said he favored equal rights for women. The Republican platform called for a constitutional amendment that would ban abortions. It opposed the use of quotas for minority groups in school admissions and employment.

Carter supported the ERA. He said he opposed abortion, but he was against a constitutional amendment banning it. The Democratic platform was in favor of programs for minority groups.

▶ **THE FINAL CAMPAIGN**

As September approached, Anderson remained an important factor in the race. He had chosen Patrick Lucey, a former Democratic governor of Wisconsin, as his running mate. Their platform was generally conservative on economic issues and liberal on social issues. Carter forces were particularly worried about Anderson. They feared he would attract voters who would normally choose the Democratic candidate.

The League of Women Voters organized televised debates between the main presidential candidates, inviting Anderson to participate in the first debate. But Carter refused to participate if Anderson were included. He said the first debate should be a two-man encounter between the major party candidates. Carter's argument was rejected. On September 21, Reagan and Anderson debated. Both men picked up support as a result of the debate. But as the election drew nearer, Anderson's support seemed to gradually decrease.

A two-man debate between Carter and Reagan was finally held on October 28. Carter focused on the issues of war and peace. Reagan focused on the economy. The debate was one of many events in the two men's hectic schedules. At stop after stop during the final days of the campaign, Reagan and Carter repeated their messages to the voters.

▶ HOW THE COUNTRY VOTED

In the November 4 election, only 52.4 percent of the Americans eligible to vote actually did so. It was the lowest turnout in a presidential election since 1948. Reagan received 51 percent of the vote; Carter received 41 percent; Anderson received 7 percent. Reagan led in 44 states and thus received those states' 489 electoral votes (a majority of electoral votes—270 votes—is needed to become president). Carter carried only the District of Columbia and six states, for 49 electoral votes. Anderson and the other candidates did not win any states.

The Republican victory spread far beyond the White House. The Republicans picked up twelve seats in the Senate, to obtain a majority for the first time since the 1950's. In the House of Representatives, they gained 33 seats, but the Democrats still retained a majority. The Republicans also gained four governorships.

Why did voters turn to Reagan and the rest of the Republican ticket? Many people said they were unhappy with Carter's performance. Some election analysts said that people's unhappiness with the economy probably hurt Carter more than any other issue.

Will Reagan be able to get the economy moving again? Will he be able to improve America's position in the world? Will he be able to cut federal spending and decrease U.S. reliance on imported fuels? These are just a few of the challenges that faced Reagan as he prepared to take office.

HOW THE COUNTRY VOTED
(The numbers are each state's electoral college votes—270 were needed to win.)

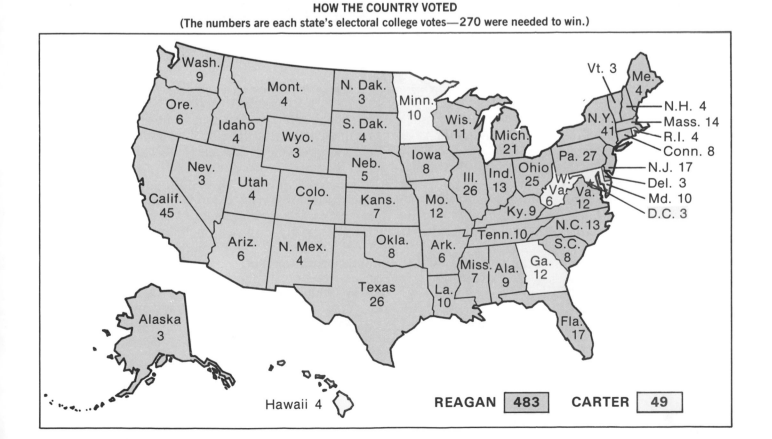

REAGAN 483   CARTER 49

YOU ARE WHAT YOU EAT

Carol never skips a meal. She is a number of pounds overweight, but her doctor says that she is undernourished.

Bill eats lots of snacks after school, and his teeth have lots of cavities. Mary also snacks, but she doesn't have any cavities.

Marty's father loves fried foods. But his doctor says that he must cut out these foods or risk having a heart attack.

Sarah's mother puts lots of salt in her food. But all that salt has given Sarah's mother high blood pressure.

All these people, like most people in North America, get enough to eat. But eating enough is not the same as eating wisely.

More and more evidence indicates that what people eat affects their health. Many people eat too much meat, too many dairy products, and too many processed foods. They are taking in too much fat, cholesterol, sugar, and salt—and too many calories. These people are increasing their chances of becoming victims of deadly diseases, including heart disease, stroke, high blood pressure, diabetes, and certain cancers.

▶ WHAT SHOULD I EAT?

Your body needs more than 50 different chemicals to grow and be healthy. These chemicals are called nutrients. They can be put into six basic groups: proteins, carbohydrates, fats, vitamins, minerals, and water.

Each nutrient has specific jobs to do in your body. These jobs cannot be done by any other nutrient. Thus, eating extra vitamin C will not make up for a shortage of vitamin D.

All the nutrients can be found in food. But different foods contain different types and amounts of nutrients. To obtain all the nutrients you need, you must eat a variety of different types of foods.

In 1980 the United States Government issued dietary guidelines. These guidelines tell you what to eat to be healthy:

- Eat a variety of foods every day.
- Maintain ideal weight.
- Avoid too much fat, saturated fat, and cholesterol.
- Eat foods that contain adequate starch and fiber.
- Avoid too much sugar.
- Avoid too much sodium (salt).

Consider the first guideline—eat a variety of foods every day. Your diet should include a selection of the following:

Fruits and vegetables. These give you vitamins A and C, carbohydrates, and fiber, among other things. Fiber is a part of plants, like the stringy part of celery. It is not digestible—that is, it passes through the body without being broken down. Fiber contains very few nutrients, but it is valuable because it helps move food materials and wastes through the digestive system.

Remember, different foods provide differ-

SUGAR IS SWEET BUT NOT SO NEAT!

Sugar causes cavities and tooth decay. As the U.S. Department of Agriculture points out in its 1979 Yearbook, this is a serious problem. One dentist explains the problem like this: If all 100,000 dentists in the United States worked day and night for a year filling cavities, there would still be as many new cavities to fill at the end of the year as when they began.

On the average, each American eats more than 130 pounds (59 kilograms) of sugar and sweeteners a year. Not all this sugar comes from candies, cakes, and other desserts. Many processed foods—including soup, cheese, salad dressing, spaghetti sauce, and even frankfurters—contain sugar.

Eating too much sugar causes other problems besides cavities. Sugar is so highly refined that it gets digested very quickly. It doesn't stay in your stomach very long. That means you may want to keep on eating. What happens then? You suddenly discover you're overweight.

Still another problem with sugar is that it contains "empty calories." It has no vitamins, no minerals, and no protein.

You don't have to stop eating sugar and sugary foods. But it wouldn't hurt to cut down. You'll discover that your desire for sweet things is partly a matter of habit. If you cut down on sugar for several weeks, you'll get used to eating less sugar. And when you go to the dentist, you will probably have fewer cavities.

ent amounts of each nutrient. Therefore it's important to vary the fruits and vegetables you choose.

Bread and cereal. These foods are rich in some of the B vitamins and in iron. If possible, eat whole grain breads and cereals. They contain fiber and many important minerals that aren't found in refined breads and cereals, even the enriched and fortified ones.

Milk, cheese, and yogurt. These foods give you calcium and several vitamins.

Meat, poultry, fish, eggs, and dried beans and peas. These foods provide protein, iron, zinc, and certain B vitamins.

Then there are foods that provide mainly calories. It would be wise to cut down on these—candy, cookies, pies, french fries, potato chips, and other sweet or fatty foods. Instead, plan to get most of your calories from other foods. By doing this, you will get not only the calories but also the important nutrients that you need.

▶ TURNING CALORIES INTO POUNDS

How many calories do you need in one day? It depends on how active you are. A fairly active 12-year-old needs between 2,200 and 2,800 calories a day. If you are very active you will need more. Some teenagers who participate in sports need more than 4,000 calories a day. Some men who play basketball with the Boston Celtics eat as many as 8,000 to 10,000 calories a day while they are at training camp.

If you eat more calories than your body can use, you will gain weight. This is easy to do, especially if you don't get much exercise. For example, a hamburger-with-everything-on-it from your favorite fast-food restaurant contains about 600 calories. Add a serving of french fries, a soda, and an apple turnover, and you've eaten more than 1,200 calories in one meal. You must eat lightly during the rest of the day, or you will gain weight.

On the other hand, if you eat fewer calories than your body uses, you will lose weight. Many young people find that they have put on too much weight. They decide to go on a diet. But while dieting, a person still needs the same amounts of vitamins and minerals. That's why it's very important that people who want to lose weight choose foods that are low in calories but that provide all the nutrients needed for good health. It's no fun ending up skinny if you get sick at the same time.

▶ SNACKING—GOOD OR BAD?

It's the middle of the afternoon—or late at night—or two hours before lunch. You're feeling hungry. You decide to have a snack, even though you've probably been told a hundred times that you shouldn't eat between meals.

Is snacking really so bad? Not necessarily. The problem isn't snacking. It's what you eat when you snack. Do you choose such foods as milk, fruit, and raw vegetables? Or do you choose "junk" foods?

Many snack foods are called junk foods because they have no—or very little—nutritional value. They are filled with "empty calories." This means they contain lots of calories but little else of value. They don't contain vitamins, minerals, and proteins. If you fill up on these foods, you don't have room in your stomach for the foods you need. Or, if you eat the foods you need—plus the junk foods—you will probably end up eating too many calories and too much sugar, fat, and salt.

So the next time you want to snack, pick up an orange or a carrot instead of a cookie or a candy. Have a glass of juice instead of a glass of soda. And if it's almost time for dinner, don't snack. Have a glass of water if you're thirsty, but don't let a snack ruin your appetite for a well-balanced meal.

▶ MAKE YOUR OWN FOODS

Perhaps you're getting the feeling that you should never eat another cookie. Things aren't as bad as that. Just like snacks, there are good cookies and bad cookies. Good cookies are relatively low in sugar. They contain things like oatmeal, raisins, nuts, and dates.

Try making your own cookies. Follow a recipe the first time. The next time, decrease the amount of sugar that the recipe calls for. With many cookie and cake recipes, you'll discover that the amount of sugar can be cut by one-third or even one-half—and you'll still produce delicious treats.

The same is true for the amount of salt that you use in your food. Don't cut salt out. Just use less of it.

Here are some other tips: Make your own salad dressing from oil, vinegar, and herbs.

Use whole wheat flour when you make pancakes. Try a yogurt and fresh fruit shake. When you buy cereal, check the ingredients on the package. Choose a cereal that's low in sugar and salt.

Checking the ingredients of the foods you buy is always a smart thing to do. Was that shake you had yesterday a milk shake, made with milk or ice cream? Or was it a fake shake, made from vegetable oil, nonfat milk solids, emulsifiers, flavorings, and sugar?

Finally, if you want to splurge on a rich, gooey dessert, go ahead. But balance the high sugar by cutting down your sugar intake during the next day or two. If you eat a heavily salted food one day, decrease your salt intake for the next few days. If you eat a fast-food lunch high in fat but low in fruits and vegetables, eat a dinner that supplies the needed nutrients.

Remember, you are what you eat. Eat a well-balanced, nutritious diet, and you will look and feel healthy. It's the best thing you can do for yourself . . . today, tomorrow, and for the rest of your life.

Many snack foods are considered "junk foods" because they contain lots of calories but little else of value.

FUN FOOD FACTS

Here are some facts about foods that may surprise you, your family, and your friends.

BIG EATERS

Babe Ruth once ate 20 hot dogs just before playing a baseball game. But a young woman in Philadelphia ate even more. On July 12, 1977, 21-year-old Linda Kuerth ate 23 frankfurters in 3 minutes 10 seconds. These were regular-sized franks.

It took more than one person to eat the largest sausage ever made. The sausage was made in England in May, 1979. It was 2 miles (3.2 kilometers) long and weighed 2,740 pounds (1,243 kilograms)! The sausage was cooked by Scouts and served at a children's party in London's Hyde Park.

WHAT'S IN A NAME?

Where did foods originally come from? The answer may not be easy to discover. Consider these familiar foods: Italian pasta actually originated in China. French croissants (rolls) were first made in Hungary. The Irish potato is a native of South and Central America. And the good old American hamburger got its start in Germany—in a town called Hamburg.

TOMATO TALES

The fact that we eat and enjoy tomatoes is due, in part, to a man named Colonel Robert G. Johnson. For years many people believed that if you ate a tomato, you would die before morning. Colonel Johnson decided to prove they were wrong.

On September 26, 1820, at noon, Colonel Johnson stood on the courthouse steps in Salem, New Jersey. In front of hundreds of people he ate a whole basketful of tomatoes.

Many people thought Johnson had gone crazy—until, that is, he not only lived but didn't even get sick.

In 1801, Thomas Jefferson became the third president of the United States. But 20 years earlier, Jefferson was one of the first people in the United States to grow tomatoes. But he grew them as a decoration—not for eating.

MILK MACHINES

The average cow produces 62 glasses of milk a day. The record-holder is a cow in Indiana. In 1975 she gave more milk in one day than any other cow ever has—372 glasses. Just imagine how tired that prize-winning cow must have been after her record milk-producing day!

CHICKEN FACTS

There are more chickens in the world today than there are people. And the chicken population is growing faster than the human population. This is because people are eating more and more chickens. Forty years ago, Americans ate about half a pound (0.2 kilograms) of chicken a year. Now they eat an average of about 37 pounds (17 kilograms) of chicken a year.

Not all chickens are raised for their meat. Some are raised to produce eggs. Forty years ago, the average egg-laying hen laid 100 eggs a year. Things have really changed. Today, an average hen lays about 240 eggs a year.

YOU'VE GOT WATER IN YOUR HEAD

Your body is more than half water. Your blood, for instance, is 90 percent water. Your brain is 75 percent water. And there is water in every one of your cells.

You lose about 2½ quarts (2.4 liters) of water a day. Some is lost as urine. Some, as perspiration. Some, when you breathe. But water is usually easy to replace. Every time you eat food, you eat water.

Can you name some foods that contain a lot of water? You probably guessed tomatoes, oranges, and watermelon. But did you know that bread is more than one-third water? Meat is more than half water. And, of course, milk and juice are nearly all water—plus natural flavoring and nutrients.

FOOD FIRSTS

The first public bakery was opened in Rome, Italy, in 171 B.C. Its specialty was a wheat-honey loaf.

Milk chocolate was first made in Vevey, Switzerland, in 1876. Credit goes to Daniel Peter, who believed that adding milk to anything would make it taste better.

Lemonade was first made in Paris, France, in 1603.

The first pizzeria in the United States opened in New York City in 1905.

Apricots were the first fruits planted in California.

KNOW YOUR BODY

What *really* happens to your body when you eat a candy bar? When you don't eat enough iron? When you exercise regularly? When you put on too much weight?

Young people are learning the answers to questions such as these through a program called Know Your Body (KYB). KYB was developed by the American Health Foundation and is being used in a number of schools throughout the United States. An international KYB program is being used in sixteen other countries.

KYB's goal is to teach what *you* can do for your body to keep it healthy. The program begins with a health questionnaire and physical examination, which screen you for "risk factors." Risk factors are health conditions or habits that can lead to disease. Risk factors include cigarette smoking, poor nutritional habits, and inadequate exercise.

During the examination, your height, weight, and blood pressure are measured. Your heart rate is measured before and after you exercise. A sample of your blood is taken. This is sent to a laboratory, which measures the amount of cholesterol and the amount of sugar in the blood. It also determines what percentage of your blood is made up of red blood cells.

The results of all the tests are put on a Health Passport. The passport is yours to keep. You can look at your score for each test and compare it to what is considered the "normal value" for that test.

If your score on one or more of the tests is too high or too low, you are encouraged to try to change the score. Most of these scores can be changed just by improving some of your health habits. For example, let's consider cholesterol. Cholesterol is a fatty substance. Your body uses some cholesterol. But if you eat foods that contain a lot of cholesterol, the extra cholesterol may stick to the walls of blood vessels. Slowly, over the years, the cholesterol builds up until it clogs the vessels. It prevents blood from flowing through the vessels, and this may cause a heart attack or a stroke.

If your cholesterol level is too high, you can lower it by changing your eating habits. What changes do you think you should make? (Hint: red meats, eggs, and ice cream are some foods that are high in cholesterol.)

What you eat, how much you exercise, and cigarette smoking affect your health. They affect your weight, the composition of your blood, the strength of your muscles, your heart rate, and the health of your lungs. If your diet is well balanced, if you exercise regularly, and if you don't smoke, your Health Passport scores will probably be very good. Even more important, you will increase your chances of living a long and healthy life.

TRACEE TALAVERA— A TERRIFIC TUMBLER

Tracee Talavera, a young American gymnast, is a rising star. And she has talent and courage that no amount of disappointment seems to shake.

This tiny athlete (about 5 feet, or 150 centimeters, tall) first entered the sports spotlight at the American Cup gymnastics competition held in New York in March, 1979. In that meet Tracee surprised everyone by winning the events on the balance beam and the uneven parallel bars and by placing third in the all-around. She was so good that her coach wanted her to enter the world championships in December. She made the American team but was kept out of the meet because she was 12 years old—one year too young to qualify.

Tracee was disappointed, but she kept on training and competing. And in March, 1980, she entered the American Cup for the second time. This time she placed first in the all-around competition, beating some of the world's best gymnasts. Tracee was exceptionally good in the uneven parallel bars; the balance beam competition, in which she did sprightly tumbling along a 4-inch (10-centimeter) wide beam; and the floor exercise, in which she combined energetic tumbling with a whimsical pantomime to the song "Whistle While You Work."

But even as Tracee trained for the American Cup, she saw that her hope of entering the 1980 Summer Olympics in Moscow was flickering out. And in April, the United States announced its decision to boycott the Summer Games. No American athlete went to Moscow, and once again Tracee suffered a big disappointment.

In December, 1981, the pixyish gymnast will finally be old enough to enter the world championships. She was expected to perform there with her usual energy and grace —perhaps even adding to her roster of wins with a top score in this major world competition that is held every other year.

Tracee first thought about being a champion gymnast back in 1972, when she and her older sister Coral watched the Soviet gymnast Olga Korbut perform amazing feats in that year's Olympics, broadcast on television. Tracee was only 5 at the time, but both girls rushed out into the yard to see how well they could imitate Olga. Soon both girls began to go to regular gymnastics classes. When Tracee was 9, the family decided that the girls should live at a gymnastics training academy in Eugene, Oregon—a nine-hour drive from the Talavera home in Walnut Creek, California. The schedule at the academy was tough, and after six months Coral quit and turned to ballet. But Tracee stayed on at the academy, working hard and seeing her family only on visits and holidays.

Tracee loves gymnastics, and her deep interest is what makes her perform better and better every year. Watch for her at the 1984 Olympics. You may just see Tracee tumble her way to a gold medal.

TRAILER TROUBLE

Donald Duck hopped out of his car and called to his nephews Huey, Dewey, and Louie, "Ah, there you are kids. All ready to go?"

Huey, Dewey, and Louie looked at Donald's car with dismay. "Gosh, Uncle Donald! What's *that?*"

"How do you like it, boys? A trailer equipped with every modern convenience. It's the only way to go camping these days."

"But we wanted to go camping in the old-fashioned way," Huey said, "with just our Junior Woodchuck camping gear."

"Yeah, Uncle Donald," Dewey added. "We want to earn our merit badges and be members of the J.W.L.O.C.R.I.W.E."

"The what?"

"The Junior Woodchuck Loyal Order of Camping and Roughing It in the Wilderness Experts," Huey explained.

"Oh, all right. Stow your old-fashioned gear and let's get this show on the road!" scoffed Donald.

The kids put their gear in the trailer, then got in the back seat of Donald's car. Donald started the car, and off they went.

Soon Donald and the boys were heading toward the mountains, away from the city traffic and crowded sidewalks.

Finally they stopped at a remote campsite.

"Well, boys," Donald sighed, "after a full day of driving, I'm ready for a hot meal and a relaxing evening in front of my television set."

"We're going to set up our camp," Huey said.

"That's not for me!" Donald said. "I'm sleeping in my cozy trailer under an electric blanket, like a modern camper."

Donald busied himself inside his trailer. He opened cans of food with his electric can opener. He heated the food on his electric stove. And while all this was going on, he watched a rerun of *Ducksmoke* on the trailer TV.

Meanwhile, the kids had put up a tent,

rolled out their sleeping bags, and started a nice little campfire.

"Dinner's ready!" Donald proclaimed from the door of the trailer. "Hot dogs, beans, and root beer."

"Aw, gee, Uncle Donald! We wanted to fix dinner over our campfire." The kids were obviously disappointed.

"Nonsense," Donald said. "This modern trailer has helped me prepare dinner in half the time you'd be able to do it in the old-fashioned way. Now quit grumbling and come and get it!"

As they were finishing their hot dogs, the trailer lights dimmed. As they were finishing their beans, the trailer lights flickered. And just as they were finishing their root beer, the trailer lights went out!

The first voice out of the darkness was Huey's: "What happened to the lights?"

"There must be something wrong with the electrical wiring," Donald answered, fumbling in the darkness for the light switch. "Ouch!" He stubbed his toe. "Oof!" He banged his head.

"Uncle Donald," suggested Dewey, "we have a kerosene lamp outside. I'll get it for you so you can see where you're going." He reached outside for the lamp and handed it to Donald.

"Hmmmf!" Donald snorted. "Such primitive equipment. I'll only need it for a minute. I'll have this problem fixed in no time at all."

The boys left their uncle peering at the fuse box in the dim lantern light and returned to their campfire.

Soon, out of the darkness came Donald, the light from the lantern flickering on the ground ahead of him.

"Doggone stupid contraption! Of all the dumb things to happen!"

"What's wrong, Uncle Donald?" asked Louie.

"The doggone battery in the trailer is dead," fumed Donald, "and I wanted to watch television. And how will I keep warm tonight? There's no power for my electric blanket."

Donald was frantic. "And how will I open cans without my electric can opener? And how will I cook breakfast if the electric stove doesn't work?"

"Now, calm down, Uncle Donald," Huey soothed. "Tomorrow morning you can take the car back to town and get a new battery for the trailer."

"I guess that's what I'll have to do," sighed Donald. "In the meantime, all I can do is get ready for bed." And he stomped off.

An instant later, the boys heard a loud "Oh, no!" It was followed immediately by the banging of the trailer door.

Joining the boys once more, Donald sat down and gazed dejectedly at the fire. "I knocked the coffee pot off the stove and spilled coffee all over my bunk!"

"Here, Uncle Donald," said Huey, holding out a toasted marshmallow on a stick. "Try my campfire special."

Still brooding over his bad luck, Donald reached absentmindedly for the sizzling marshmallow.

"YEOW!"

"Careful, Uncle Donald," Huey warned, a little too late. "They're awful hot."

"Thanks a lot," Donald mumbled, his scorched finger in his mouth. "I'm going to turn in before anything else happens."

"Do you want to sleep out here, Uncle Donald?" Louie asked. "We've got an extra sleeping bag."

"Not me! I'm sleeping in the car tonight. If I can't look at TV, at least I can listen to the car radio."

Donald marched toward the car, opened the door, and climbed in.

The mountain air was getting cooler, so Louie threw another log on the fire and settled into his sleeping bag. Huey and Dewey crawled into their sleeping bags, too. In a moment, the three campers were fast asleep.

Inside the car, Donald switched on the radio. Soothed by the strains of the Duckburg Symphony, he leaned back on the seat and closed his eyes.

Donald woke up the next morning to the smell of sizzling bacon and the voice of his nephew Huey: "Wake up, Uncle Donald! Breakfast is ready."

Donald sat up on the car seat and stretched. Outside he could see the kids cooking breakfast over a campfire.

"Come on, Uncle Donald. Have some bacon and eggs."

Donald climbed out of the car. "No, thanks, boys," he said, rather smugly. "I'm going to wait until I get my new camper battery. Then I can cook up a real gourmet breakfast for myself."

Donald watched his nephews clean up after breakfast. "When I get my battery, you'll have plenty of hot water to wash those dishes, instead of heating water over the fire."

"We don't mind, Uncle Donald," said Huey.

"Well," his uncle said, walking toward the car, "I guess we should be getting to town. It's a long drive."

Donald and the kids piled into the car. Donald put the key in the ignition and turned it to "start." Nothing happened. He tried it again. Nothing happened again. The car battery was as dead as a doornail.

"I don't believe it!" moaned Donald. "Why did this happen to *me?*"

"Maybe because *you* left the car radio on all night and wore out the battery," Huey suggested.

"This is terrible," Donald groaned. "Miles from civilization! Without a car! Without an electric stove! Without even an electric blanket! We're doomed!"

"Take it easy, Uncle Donald," Huey said.

"The first rule of the J.W.L.O.C.R.I.W.E. is 'DON'T PANIC!' "

"We'll just have to hike to town," Louie added.

"But I don't even know what direction town is!" Donald squawked.

The valiant trio of Junior Woodchuck Loyal Order of Camping and Roughing It in the Wilderness Experts smiled confidently.

"Just follow us," Dewey said.

Since he didn't have much choice in the matter, Donald followed his nephews into the woods.

"The town is due east," Louie directed.

"And which way is *that?*" Donald asked.

Dewey pointed to the sunrise. "The sun rises in the east," he explained.

"Oh."

By midday, Donald was starved and exhausted. "Hold it, boys," he gasped. "I've got to rest."

He made his way through tall brush, looking for a spot to sit down.

Suddenly, he felt himself sliding down a steep embankment. "Yeow!" he shrieked. The nephews ran over to the embankment and looked down. There was Uncle Donald, sitting at the bottom of the hill, holding his ankle and bellowing like a bull.

"I think you've sprained your ankle, Uncle," Dewey said, examining Donald's foot. "We'll have to carry you."

"How are you going to do that?" Donald asked grumpily. "You'll need a stretcher."

"Just leave that to us," Huey answered. "Dewey and Louie, go find two long poles. I'll dip my kerchief in the stream over there and wrap it around Uncle Donald's ankle."

The poles were found, and Donald's ankle was bandaged with Huey's kerchief. The kids made a stretcher out of the poles and their shirts. They lifted Donald onto the stretcher and continued their journey out of the woods.

In another two hours, the brave band of Junior Woodchucks marched into town with their unfortunate uncle.

A week later, the trailer was back in the garage, Donald was back on his feet, and the three boys had been awarded their J.W.L.O.C.R.I.W.E. merit badges.

"I'm sorry I spoiled your camping trip, boys," Donald said apologetically.

"You didn't spoil anything, Uncle Donald," Huey said.

"We never would have won our merit badges *without* you," Louie added.

And Dewey chimed in, "Going camping with you proved we could handle *any* emergency in the woods!"

PARK OF MONSTERS

Imagine that you're walking through a rocky, wooded glen. Tired, you clamber onto a mossy boulder and sit down. Suddenly, with a shock, you realize that this is no simple rock—you're sitting on the knee of a stone monster!

In Italy, north of Rome, there is a garden filled with these strange stone beings. Called the Park of Monsters, it was designed in the 1500's by an Italian prince, Vicino Orsini. Over the years, trees, vines, and bushes covered the huge figures, and the garden was forgotten. Then, about 30 years ago, the trees were pruned back and the garden was opened to visitors.

About a dozen truly monstrous figures loom up from behind trees or around bends in the paths. There are also other fanciful statues, a tilted room, and a miniature temple.

Most of the figures are carved from natural rock outcroppings. Some—like one of a woman balancing a bowl of greenery on her head—seem to mock the graceful lines of classical sculpture. Others look like giants or trolls that have stepped out of a fairy tale and suddenly turned to stone. But all the figures are harmless. If you visit the garden, you may touch, climb, and in some cases even walk inside the monsters.

59

STRIKE IT RICH!

"Gold!"

It was a magic word. It made people leave their homes, their jobs, their families. They packed a few belongings and set out across a huge continent. They endured desert heat, hunger, disease, and the threat of outlaws. Many of them died. But more kept coming, all driven by the hope of finding gold.

Gold rushes are part of the history of North America. In 1849, 80,000 people poured into California. Most of these "Forty-niners," as they were called, headed into the area around the American River, north and east of Sacramento. Gold had first been found there in January, 1848. The Forty-niners staked their claims and dug, mined, and panned for gold. Few struck it rich, but many of them settled in California and thus helped to open up the Far West. In 1850, California became a state.

In 1858, 25,000 prospectors rushed to the Fraser River in British Columbia after a gold strike there. The next year, the "Fifty-niners" followed the call of gold to Colorado. And beginning in 1897, the Yukon and Alaska became the scenes of the last great gold rushes in North America. Even the severe cold couldn't stop those who dreamed of finding the precious yellow metal.

Most of the prospectors failed. But for some, the dreams of discovery came true. Great fortunes were made. In 1852, $80,000,000 worth of gold was unearthed in California. Even today, almost 130 years later, there are gold prospectors still dreaming of the "big strike"—especially because we are now seeing a tremendous increase in the value of gold.

In the 1850's, gold was worth about $16 an ounce. Over a century later, it was worth about $35 an ounce. In the 1970's, gold prices began to steadily climb, and in 1980 the price of an ounce skyrocketed to over $800. It settled back to about $625, still an enormous sum. Because of the fantastic prices, people are showing a new interest in finding gold. There has been no 1849-style gold rush, but prospectors are once again searching for gold along the banks of the American River, as well as many other streams in North America.

YOU CAN PAN FOR GOLD

Prospecting is not easy. It can take a long time and it offers no guarantee of success. Good luck is often more important than how long or how hard you work. An experienced prospector may find next to nothing in a year of looking for gold; a newcomer may strike pay dirt the first day out. But you won't find anything unless you look, and the panning method is probably the cheapest and simplest way to start prospecting.

As a river or stream flows past a vein of gold, it may break off small bits and flakes of the metal and carry them along in its current. But gold is very heavy—almost twenty times as heavy as water—so the little particles will sink to the stream bed wherever the current slows down.

The best place to pan for gold, then, is a spot where the stream runs slowly. This may be at the inside of a curve in the stream, close to the edge. If you toss a twig or a leaf into the water, you can follow it along to find the spots where the current is losing speed. These would be good locations to start panning.

You'll probably get wet, so it's a good idea to wear waterproof boots. And of course, any water can be dangerous, so always proceed with caution.

THE METHOD

With your shovel, dig as deep as you can into the stream bed. Fill your pan about half full with dirt. Carefully place the pan into the water and shake it a bit. This will move the dirt around and allow the much heavier gold to settle toward the bottom of the pan.

Continue to stir the gravel around in the water, and tip the pan slightly so that the water slowly spills out. Gradually all the light dirt will be washed away, and you will be left with small pebbles and sand—and possibly bits of gold.

You can pick out the pebbles with your fingers and toss them away. Continue dipping the pan in the water and washing away the dirt. Finally you will be left with only fine black sand. If you find no black sand, you will find no gold. Black sand and gold always occur together.

With your tweezers, sift through the black sand that is left. Look for tiny yellow grains

THE EQUIPMENT

If you would like to try panning, you will need the right equipment. The most important implement is the pan. A piepan will do, but it should be made of a heavy metal like tin to keep its shape. Hard plastic pans, made especially for gold hunters, are also suitable.

You should also have a shovel or a small garden spade, tweezers for picking tiny flakes of gold out of the dirt you examine, and a small bottle to put your gold in—if you really strike it rich!

of gold. Don't be fooled by fool's gold. Fool's gold is pyrite, a mineral that is yellow, like real gold, but much harder. Real gold is soft and you can easily press into it or flatten it with your tweezers. Fool's gold will break when you push into it with tweezers or hit it with a hammer.

If you find gold, or something you think is gold, put it into your small bottle and put the cover on tight. Later, if you wish, you can take your gold to an assay office, where it will be tested. The assayer will tell you if you have found real gold.

If you don't find any gold, don't give up your search. There may be some nuggets at the next bend in the stream, or beneath a tree at the water's edge where the current slows to a lazy crawl.

Try panning for gold. You just may strike it rich!

STAKING A CLAIM

If luck is with you and you do strike gold, you should immediately stake a claim. A mining claim gives you, and only you, the right to pan for gold at the location of your strike.

First you should put up a sign at your panning site stating that that area is your claim. Then you must find out who owns the property that you are mining on.

If the land is owned by a private individual, you would have to get his or her permission to work the claim. And the owner would probably want some payment in return for allowing you to work the land. If the land is public, you should contact your local, state, provincial, or national government to find out how to make your mining claim.

Good luck!

ACID RAIN

Not too many years ago, people who wanted pure water would collect rain in big wooden barrels. But now, the water that collects in a rain barrel is likely to be anything but pure. In fact, it may be very much like vinegar.

Vinegar is an acid. And in more and more parts of the world, the rain and snow that fall from the skies contain acid—acid that kills plants and animals, erodes buildings, and may even harm people.

The problem is caused by power plants and other industries that burn oil and, especially, coal. Cars, buses, and other vehicles that use petroleum-based fuels are also to blame. When coal and oil are burned, sulfur dioxide and nitrogen oxides are produced as wastes. These chemicals enter the atmosphere. They combine with oxygen in the atmosphere to produce sulfuric acid and nitric acid.

Winds may carry the acids thousands of miles from their source. Acids that originate in Ohio may eventually be part of the rain that falls on Quebec. Acids from Ontario may fall on New York. Acids produced in Britain and France may fall on Sweden.

Acid rain seems to cause the greatest damage in lakes and rivers. As these bodies of water become more and more acid, the plants and animals that live there die. Eggs do not hatch. Bacteria that break down dead leaves and other organic matter also die.

People who fished the lakes and rivers of eastern North America were among the first to notice that something strange was happening. Places that used to provide large catches were no longer teeming with fish. People could spend a whole day at their favorite fishing spot and not even get a nibble. When scientists began to study the lakes and rivers, they discovered that the water was too acid to support life. Eventually, they traced the acid back to the industries and cars.

In the Adirondack Mountains of New York, more than 200 lakes have become fishless. In Ontario, 140 lakes are without fish—and the fish in 48,000 other lakes are threatened. In Nova Scotia, 7 rivers that once teemed with salmon now have no fish at all.

Will the situation improve? Not unless some action is taken. More and more sulfur dioxide and nitrogen oxides are being produced. Methods of removing these chemicals from factory smoke and car exhausts are expensive and not always effective. So it seems that there may be increasing amounts of acid in rain.

Many people think acid rain is one of the most serious environmental problems in North America. In 1980, Canada and the United States agreed to work together to control its spread. As one concerned official put it: "What goes up must come down. With acid rain, however, what comes down is much worse than what went up."

THE UNDERWATER WORLD
OF A CORAL REEF

Hugging the low shoreline of jagged coral rock, a boat chugs through the transparent, turquoise waters of the Caribbean. The boat, with a small group of divers aboard, is headed toward the Mexican island of Cozumel. As it travels southward, small greenish brown patches of coral growth become visible beneath the water. A school of dolphins mysteriously appears off the bow. Diving over and under one another, the dolphins playfully try to get the best position to ride the wave of water pushed forward by the boat's prow. A sea turtle lazily basking on the surface is startled by the engines. It swims off with great flapping thrusts of its powerful front legs. Several flying fish suddenly pop out of the water and go skimming off across the surface. They glide for some distance until they lose speed and plop back into the sea.

Nearing the southern end of the island, the boat angles away from shore and moves out into deeper water. The boat soon comes to a stop, and the anchor is dropped over the side. The divers have arrived at their destination. Beneath the ocean's surface, but visible through the clear water, is Palancar Reef—one of the most spectacular coral reefs in the Caribbean. The divers will now enter a fantastic underwater world, a world that is at the same time both beautiful and eerie.

But what are corals, and how do they help make a coral reef?

Brain coral

Star coral

Staghorn coral

▶ **THE REEF BUILDERS**

Although corals may appear to be exotic plant life, they are actually the skeletons of tiny sea animals called coral polyps. The skeletons of billions of certain kinds of corals make up a coral reef.

Corals belong to the same family as sea anemones and jellyfish. The body of a coral polyp is tubular, and it has a mouth surrounded by tiny tentacles. Its limestone skeleton grows outside its body and usually takes the shape of a cup. The cup protects the coral just as a shell protects a crab. During the day, the tentacles rest in the cup. At night, they reach out to search for small prey and push the food into the polyp's mouth.

Each kind of coral takes a form that is different in size and shape. Some shapes resemble tree branches, flowers, or mushrooms. Many corals have been named for the fascinating patterns they form—such as brain coral, star coral, hat coral, and staghorn coral. It is the colors of the living coral polyps that give color to the skeletons—red, green, orange, blue, yellow.

Most corals live together in colonies. When the polyp dies, its skeleton remains part of the colony. And as more and more coral skeletons pile up, they may form the base of a coral reef. The reef will continue to grow upward and out, very slowly, only a few inches a year at the most. But over centuries, a reef can grow to tremendous proportions. A reef may be made up of many thousands of coral colonies, created by billions of individual polyps. The only living part of the reef is the top layer of coral polyps.

▶ **KINDS OF CORAL REEFS**

Corals are found in all the oceans of the world. But the true reef-forming corals live in the warm, clear waters of the tropics. They cannot live in waters that are colder than 65°F (18°C).

There are three types of coral reefs—fringing reefs, barrier reefs, and atolls.

A fringing reef is found in shallow water and closely borders the shore.

A barrier reef is much farther out from the shore and is separated from the shore by wide channels of water. It forms a barrier between the water near the shore and the

open sea. The most famous such reef is the Great Barrier Reef, off the northeastern coast of Australia. It is about 1,250 miles (2,000 kilometers) long. Palancar, also a barrier reef, is only 6 miles (10 kilometers) in length.

An atoll is found in the open sea and is unconnected with any land mass. It forms a ring of low coral islands and encircles a body of water called a lagoon. There are hundreds of atolls scattered across the South Pacific.

A coral reef creates a special kind of underwater community. The coral skeletons form the reef structure. Ocean waves carry tiny plants toward the reef. The plants root and thrive on the reef, forming a cover of vegetation. This plant life provides food for fish and other creatures. And the complicated architecture of the reef offers all these creatures shelter. The reef becomes a bustling community where plants and animals depend on one another. It resembles an incredibly beautiful underwater garden, filled with oddly shaped formations and blooming with the color of the living corals and of the strange creatures that dwell there.

(A)

(B)

(C)

▶ LIFE AT PALANCAR REEF

The towering formations of Palancar Reef reach up like underwater skyscrapers from the ocean floor. Narrow, sandy canyons knife their way through the towering structures. Within the reef are the entrances of grottos, leading back into the dark recesses of the coral. Strange and colorful creatures swim through this silent, underwater world.

At Palancar, as on other coral reefs, competition for space is fierce, and many animals dwell closely together. Living with the coral polyps are such creatures as sea anemones (**A**), sponges (**B**), tube worms (**C**), and sea whips and sea fans. Sea whips and sea fans are related to corals. But rather than having hard skeletons, they have soft, horny ones.

The long, delicate arms of an orange feather star reach out from a narrow crevice (**D**). A basket star lies curled up in a tight ball far down among a sea whip's branches. In a niche of the coral is a large speckled coral crab (**E**). Peeking out from another crevice is a small goldentail moray eel. One of the reef's most familiar residents is the little arrow crab. While larger crabs hide during the day, the tiny arrow crab fearlessly clambers out in the open over the coral or pauses to rest on a convenient sponge.

The reef is teeming with brilliantly colored tropical fish. Schools of tiny blue chromis hover about the branches of the coral (**F**). Some French grunts mingle in a group near

68

the shallow edge of the reef. A zebra-striped banded butterfly fish swims leisurely past, followed by a stunning queen angelfish. Nearby, an equally striking male princess parrotfish pauses briefly at a coral head, takes a bite out of it with its beaklike front teeth, and then hurries on its way. Lurking back in the shadows of the crevices are squirrelfish and blackbar soldierfish. Quiet during the day, they will come out at night to hunt. Swimming back and forth in one small crevice is a tiny black-and-white striped spotted drum. Perfectly concealed among the branches of a sea whip, an elongated trumpetfish suddenly darts out and seizes an unsuspecting shrimp.

With the setting of the sun, the reef community undergoes a transformation. The fish and other creatures that were active during the day find a sheltered spot in the coral and settle down for the night. In turn, the squirrelfish and blackbar soldierfish move out into the open to begin their evening search for food. So do the moray eels, crabs, and octopuses. Basket stars emerge from among the branches of the sea whips and unfurl their long, netlike arms. They rotate their arms to capture microscopic animals that go drifting past in an endless stream. And all over the reef, billions of coral tentacles are extended, also gathering food. The corals will probably not live long. But their skeletons will remain, adding to the formation of the coral reef.

PETER D. CAPEN
Author and Photographer
Terra Mar Productions

(D)

(E)

(F)

WHODUNIT?

People of all ages enjoy mystery stories. Most readers love to guess "whodunit." But how good are readers as detectives? Could they solve a crime if given a chance? In 1980, a transatlantic cruise gave some mystery fans the chance to answer these questions.

Also during the year, a teenage detective named Nancy Drew was making headlines. She was celebrating the 50th anniversary of her first case.

▶ **MYSTERIES AT SEA**

In April, 1980, the MS *Sagafjord* left Port Everglades, Florida. Its destination was Genoa, Italy. On board were more than 300 passengers—and some very special guests. The guests included a London police officer, a former FBI agent, two private detectives, a mystery book writer, and a "Man of Many Aliases."

The very special guests provided the passengers with some very unusual entertainment. They gave talks on such subjects as "How to Trail a Suspect," "Self Defense Tips for Clumsy People," and "10 Fun Things to Do with Arsenic." They showed passengers how to invent disguises, change one's voice, and create an alibi.

One night there was a Policeman's Ball, and passengers came dressed as their favorite detectives. The person with the best costume won a trench coat, just like those worn by many well-known fictional detectives. The winner appeared as Miss Marple. Miss Marple never wears a trench coat, but she's a famous sleuth in Agatha Christie mysteries.

Perhaps the most fun was provided by the mysteries the passengers were given to solve. The Man of Many Aliases boarded the ship using an alias (a fake name). The passengers were to try to identify him, and they could use a lie detector and fingerprinting equipment. There were also two murders. Of course, these weren't *real* murders, but they seemed like the real thing. There were at least five suspects for each murder and some very important clues.

The first murder took place on the deck of the ship. Bunky Banister was sitting in a deck chair when someone "strangled" him with a pink silk scarf. The second victim was the lovely Hermione Gooddeed. She was "killed" in the ship's swimming pool—in front of five witnesses!

The ship's passengers who tried to solve the mysteries had a rough time of it. The suspects lied and tried to incriminate one another. There were no simple solutions. Prizes were awarded to those passengers

In 1980 the famous detective Nancy Drew celebrated the 50th anniversary of her first case.

who came up with the most original, the most logical, and the most wicked solutions.

▶ A TEENAGE DETECTIVE

In 1980, Nancy Drew was 18 years old . . . and 50 years old. Nancy is a fictional character who was created in 1930 by Edward Stratemeyer. He wrote three mysteries about the clever and independent girl detective. These first books were rewritten by Stratemeyer's daughter, Harriet Stratemeyer Adams. She went on to write 55 more Nancy Drew mysteries. Adams doesn't publish the books under her own name. She uses the pen name Carolyn Keene.

In the early books, Nancy was 16 years old. Now she is 18. This change was made so that she wouldn't break driving laws in any states. Nancy used to drive a little blue Model-A roadster, which has since been traded in for a modern car. Basically, however, Nancy hasn't changed much through the years.

Adams says, "Nancy is like a daughter who is very close to me. I guess we have grown closer as the years have gone along. Being a fictional daughter, she does exactly what I tell her to, or rather let her, do. She

never disagrees, and together we get the job done and the mystery solved."

Many of Nancy's adventures are based on Adams' own experiences and those of her children and grandchildren. "I do on-the-spot research," says Adams. "Then I exaggerate by imagining what might have happened. In Africa, I saw a baboon about to pluck off a woman's wig, and I yelled to stop him. I incorporated this into a story in which I let the baboon succeed in order to embarrass an annoying young woman."

The Nancy Drew mysteries are read all over the world. The books have been translated into over a dozen languages, including French, Dutch, Japanese, and Icelandic.

People often ask Adams how to write a good mystery. "It's simple," she says. "Catch interest on the first page and never let it wane."

And so, before you have turned very many pages in a Nancy Drew mystery book, you will find her involved in two or even three plots. Sometimes Nancy gets into trouble and must be rescued by her friends. But everything ends happily—except for the person who committed the crime. Nancy always learns "whodunit"!

SAVING ENERGY ON THE ROAD

Ten years ago, gasoline sold for 35 cents a gallon in the United States. Today it sells for about $1.35 a gallon. And no one expects the price to go down. In fact, the experts tell us that prices will go up . . . and up.

The rising cost of gasoline has had a big impact on Americans. It has affected driving habits and auto sales. The auto industry is working hard to develop cars that will use less gas. And scientists and engineers are trying to develop alternatives to gasoline and gasoline engines.

▶ **THE SHRINKING AUTOMOBILE**

Until the mid-1970's, America's favorite cars were big cars. Many people didn't care if they got only a few miles to a gallon of gasoline. Gas was plentiful and cheap. Car buyers wanted power, speed, and roominess. Manufacturers encouraged this attitude because they could make bigger profits on bigger cars.

Of course, there were some people who didn't want big cars. They preferred the smaller cars, which cost less money to buy and got better gas mileage. These people often bought foreign cars. In 1970, about 15 percent of the cars sold in the United States were foreign-made.

Then several developments occurred that caused many Americans to rethink their car-buying habits. The first development was the 1973 oil embargo by oil-producing countries in the Middle East. This temporarily cut off a major supply of crude oil to the United States. Because gasoline is made from crude oil, the result was a widespread shortage of gasoline.

The second development was a law passed by the federal government that lowered highway speed limits to 55 miles (88.5 kilometers) per hour. This made the powerful engines of big cars less important.

The third development was inflation. Prices of everything kept going up. Small cars began costing as much as big cars had cost a few years before. And big cars began to seem like unaffordable luxury items to many people.

The fourth development was another gasoline shortage, in 1979. Gas prices jumped during the shortage, and they continued to climb after supplies had returned to normal.

More and more people began to buy smaller cars. U.S. manufacturers were not making enough small cars, so people turned to European and Japanese manufacturers. In 1980, more than 25 percent of the cars sold in the United States were foreign-made.

Because U.S. manufacturers were selling

The Chevette and the Escort: 1981 American cars that promise mileage as good as that of many foreign cars.

'LIGHTER, SMALLER, COMPETITIVE, FUEL-EFFICIENT... I THINK RESEARCH AND DEVELOPMENT MAY HAVE DONE IT AGAIN!'

fewer cars, they lost money. They had to lay off workers and even close some of their manufacturing plants.

Today, U.S. manufacturers have realized that the era of big cars is over. They are spending billions of dollars to develop cars that are more fuel-efficient. By 1985, American-made cars are expected to average 28 miles per gallon (12 kilometers per liter). This is twice as much as the 1975 average.

Some of the new, smaller American cars came on the market in the fall of 1980. They give gas mileage that is comparable to that of the small imported cars.

▶ ELECTRONIC FUEL SAVERS

Smallness is not the only gas-saving improvement planned by auto makers. Better functioning engines are another. One way to accomplish this is by putting a minicomputer in a car. Some researchers believe that such a computer can cut a car's use of fuel by as much as 25 percent.

By the late 1980's almost every car is expected to contain a computer. The computer will control various engine functions.

• It will adjust the intake of fuel and air, so that the engine receives the most efficient burning mixture.

• It will control the recirculation of gases given off by the engine. This will save gas and decrease pollution.

• It will check the performance of engine parts and diagnose problems.

A computer terminal will be located on the dashboard of the car. The terminal will tell the driver if there is an engine problem. It will indicate how well the antipollution exhaust system is working, and it will indicate the tire pressure.

Computers in automobiles will have other uses, too. They might even be used by passengers to play games—such as computer chess, baseball, or space wars.

In West Germany, engineers have developed a computer system that gives a driver information about road and weather conditions. When a driver begins a trip, he or she enters the destination in the car's computer. The computer sends this information to computers installed along the roads. The roadside computers tell the car computer which is the best route to take. This information is flashed on a screen on the dashboard. As the car travels along, the roadside computers will keep it informed of any sudden changes in travel conditions, such as an accident or unexpected flooding. When this happens, the roadside computers will tell the car computer what other routes can be used.

PUT SOME CORN IN THE TANK

Because gasoline is becoming more and more expensive to use as a fuel, scientists are studying substitute fuels. At the present time, gasohol is receiving the most attention.

Gasohol is 90 percent gasoline and 10 percent alcohol. The alcohol is made from various crops, such as corn, sugarcane, and sorghum. Gasohol is being sold by more than 1,000 stations across the United States. It is particularly popular in the corn-growing areas of the Midwest.

Gasohol costs more than gasoline. But users say they get better mileage with gasohol than with gasoline. Other people disagree. They say that gasohol mileage is less. This is to be expected, they say, because alcohol does not contain as much energy as gasoline. Thus it should not provide as good mileage.

The mileage controversy has not yet been solved. In addition, the use of gasohol can cause pollution problems. Burning gasohol produces more hydrocarbon emissions than does burning gasoline. There are also maintenance problems. Researchers report that gasohol can damage rubber and plastic parts, such as tubing.

Still another problem occurs at the production end. The amount of energy used to grow corn and make gasohol is greater than the amount of energy in the gasohol. This is because energy is needed to produce fertilizers and to power tractors and harvesters. The process of converting the corn into alcohol also uses energy.

Some of these problems can probably be solved. Energy costs would decrease if garbage instead of crops were used as the alcohol source, and if the manufacturing process were improved. The U.S. Government is spending millions of dollars to support gasohol research. The hope is that gasohol will be one more way that the country can cut its dependence on imported fuel.

DON'T FILL IT, CHARGE IT

Gasoline engines aren't the only way to power an automobile. The most realistic alternative is electricity. Instead of an engine, the car has a large battery. The battery changes chemical energy into electrical energy. Eventually all the chemical energy is changed to electrical energy. When the battery needs more chemical energy, the battery can be recharged. This is simple. Just plug the battery into an electric outlet. During recharging, electricity is changed into chemical energy in the battery. In this way the battery can be used again and again.

Electric vehicles are not a new idea. In fact, at the beginning of the 20th century there were more electric cars on American roads than gasoline cars. But gasoline became plentiful, and gasoline engines were greatly improved. By the 1920's, electric cars had almost disappeared from the roads.

In the 1960's, concern over air pollution caused by gasoline engines led to renewed interest in electric cars. Several companies began to sell electric vehicles. But the range of these cars was limited. They couldn't go very far before they had to be recharged, and they couldn't go very fast.

Scientists and engineers are working on developing better batteries. In 1980, Gulf and Western Industries (G&W) announced the development of a new battery. It installed the battery in a Volkswagen. The Volkswagen was able to travel a distance of 150 miles (241 kilometers) without a recharge. G&W said that the battery could be on the market by 1984.

Another way to save energy is to use electricity instead of gasoline to power a car. This G&W van is powered by a new kind of electric battery, which could be on the market by 1984.

The G&W battery contains zinc. The battery is connected to a tank containing chlorine hydrate. When the chlorine hydrate is pumped into the battery, it reacts with the zinc to form zinc chloride. In the process, an electric current is produced. When the battery is recharged, the process is reversed. Chlorine hydrate and zinc are formed. It takes six to eight hours to recharge the G&W battery, using a regular electric outlet. This can be done at night, while the car's owner is asleep.

According to G&W, recharging the electric Volkswagen was a lot cheaper than buying gasoline. It cost about one third as much as the gas needed to drive the same distance.

Electric vehicles have other advantages in addition to saving money. They don't produce wastes that pollute the air. And they aren't as noisy as gasoline-powered cars.

Most trips that people take are relatively short. They go shopping, to work, or to school. Electric vehicles with a 150-mile range would be ideal for this kind of trip. Some analysts believe that by the end of the 20th century, 40 percent of all new cars in the United States will be battery-powered.

SMART DRIVING SAVES ENERGY

Here are six tips that will help drivers save gasoline:

1. To get the best mileage, drive at or below 55 miles (88.5 kilometers) per hour. Most cars use 20 percent less gas when driven at lower speeds than when they are driven at 70 miles (113 kilometers) per hour. That's like saving 25 cents or more on a gallon of gas.

2. Avoid quick, jackrabbit starts. They use more gas than brisk but smooth starts.

3. Avoid idling. A minute of idling uses twice as much gas as restarting the engine.

4. Keep the car tuned and in top operating condition. To get good mileage, it is important that carburetors, valves, and other engine parts be clean.

5. Keep tires properly inflated. Every two pounds (0.9 kilograms) of pressure added to non-radial tires (up to the maximum stated on the tire) increases gas mileage about 1 percent.

6. Remove unnecessary weight from the car. The lighter the car, the less fuel is needed to "push" it a certain distance.

Bibbidi– Bobbidi... Who?

Even though the sun was barely up, a lone figure worked in the kitchen of the castle. Cinderella was busily preparing breakfast for the birds and mice that had become her friends.

As she served the meal, Cinderella noticed that her two favorite mice were not there. "It's not like Jaq and Gus to be late," she said to herself, "especially when it's time to eat. Now where could they be?"

Suddenly two tiny mice tumbled into the kitchen. "So there you are," Cinderella pretended to scold. "I was just about to give your breakfast to the others."

"Cinderelly, Cinderelly! Upystairs! Stepsisties!" sputtered Jaq.

"Now, slow down. You know I can't understand you," smiled Cinderella.

As the two mice squeaked urgently, a small, plump figure in a blue hooded robe burst into the room. It was the fairy godmother! She had come to visit Cinderella.

"What shall I do? What could have happened to it?" gasped the fairy godmother. "I just don't understand. It can't have grown legs and walked away."

Poor Cinderella couldn't make sense of anything she said. "Please, all of you, settle down. Now, godmother, you first. Tell me what's wrong."

"Well, my dear, it's the strangest thing. I had my magic wand with me when I arrived, but now I can't find it. It's vanished."

"Now, now," soothed Cinderella. "Are you sure you brought the wand with you? You are rather forgetful at times. After all, as a person gets older . . ."

Before Cinderella could finish, her fairy godmother broke in. "It's true I'm no longer a novice godmother, but I'm not ready for the Old Fairies' Home yet! I'm absolutely certain I had it with me."

Jaq and Gus were still jabbering excitedly, and tugging at Cinderella's skirts.

"What are you two up to now?" asked Cinderella as Jaq and Gus pulled her toward the stairs. "Is there something up there you want me to see?"

"I wonder if they know something about my wand," suggested the fairy godmother.

76

Cinderella started for the stairs, her godmother right behind her. From Anastasia's upstairs room they could hear the sound of a terrible quarrel.

"Give it to me, Drizella. It's my turn," shrieked Anastasia. "You haven't been able to make it work. Now give me a chance."

Drizella sneered an angry reply. "Don't be so selfish. After all, whose idea was it to take the wand? Mine! So the wand is mine!"

With that, Drizella dodged away from her sister's grasp and waved the magic wand in the air. "Hobbidy-bobbidy-zoo, fill my pockets with gold."

She smirked at her sister. "There! I'm sure I've got it right now."

But when she thrust her hand into her pocket, all Drizella found was a handful of squirming goldfish. "Ugh! What's wrong with this thing? I wished for gold jewelry, not gold fish."

Anastasia snatched the wand from her greedy sister. "You can't do anything right!" She thought for a moment, then waved the wand above her head. "I wish for a beautiful fur coat. Hippity-hoppity-doo."

In a flash, a billy goat appeared before Anastasia. "I said 'coat,' " she wailed, "not 'goat.' "

Cinderella's godmother watched as the two ill-tempered sisters engaged in a tug-of-war over the wand. "Thank goodness they haven't discovered the magic words," she whispered. "We must get the wand back before they *do*. If they guess the words, the wand will grant all their greedy wishes."

Just then, the stepsisters saw Cinderella and the fairy godmother standing in the doorway. "What are you doing here?" demanded Anastasia.

"Yes," agreed Drizella. "What are you doing snooping around here? Leave us alone and tend to your own business!"

"My own business! Well! I've never heard of such a thing," huffed the feisty little godmother. "If I had my magic wand, I'd turn you into a pair of cackling crows. That's what you sound like."

"How dare you talk to us like that," shrieked Anastasia. "This isn't your wand, it's ours. We found it. And, as mother always taught us, 'Finders, keepers!' "

Cinderella tried to step in and stop the argument. "Anastasia, Drizella, you know that wand doesn't belong to you. Please return it right now!"

Drizella only laughed. "Listen to miss goody-goody. You've got everything you want—the prince, the castle, everything."

"Yeah," Anastasia chimed in. "Now it's our turn." And she slammed the door in the fairy godmother's face.

"Godmother! Are you all right?" asked Cinderella.

"Yes," replied her fairy godmother, "but we must get that wand away from them."

Cinderella opened her stepsisters' door. "Oh, no," she sighed. "They're not here. They must have gone out the other door. We'll have to search the castle. I'll take the upper floors. Godmother, you look on this floor. Jaq and Gus, you take the first floor."

The stepsisters, meanwhile, had slipped into the castle's kitchen. It was a beehive of activity. Dozens of cooks stirred and tasted under the watchful eye of the plump master chef. Underneath the table, on which the pastry cook was preparing a strawberry tart, Lucifer the cat waited hungrily to catch a stray morsel of crust.

Anastasia sniffed the wonderful aromas. "Mmm! Everything smells so good. I think I'll have something to eat."

"You're always hungry," retorted Drizella. "Well, go on, eat! And while you're making a pig out of yourself, I'm going to try one last time to make this stupid wand work. Oh, what are those magic words?"

So while Anastasia was heaping her plate with food, her sister was trying all the words she could think of: "Clippity-cloppity-boo! Snippety-snappity-loo! Pippity-poppity-poo! Oh, this is hopeless."

Drizella impatiently threw the wand to the ground. "I've had enough of this. Good riddance, and a bibbidi-bobbidi-boo to you! I think I'll have something to eat."

When the magic words were spoken, the wand sprang to life. It rose slowly into the air, filling the room with a spray of multicolored magic dust. Strange things began to happen.

Lids rose off the pots simmering on the stove and sailed through the air. Cakes rising in the ovens blew their tops.

"What's going on here?" demanded the red-faced chef. "I'm preparing a banquet for the King, and I simply won't have this kind of mischief in my kitchen."

As the stout little chef sputtered his protest, the wand lifted him off the floor and deposited him in a sink full of dishwater.

"The magic words! You finally found them!" cried Anastasia. "Tell me what they are."

"That's my secret, sister dear. But first we have to get that wand back." The stepsisters dropped their plates and chased the wand as it sailed around the kitchen.

As luck would have it, Jaq and Gus had just arrived to search the kitchen.

"Oh, no!" squeaked Jaq. "It looks like

stepsisties found magic words. Quick! We get Cinderelly.''

The kitchen staff watched in dismay as the bickering stepsisters chased the magic wand. ''Grab it,'' Anastasia ordered Drizella. ''Now that we know the magic words, we can have anything we want. We'll fix Cinderella.''

''What do you mean, 'we' know the words?'' replied Drizella as she grabbed the wand. ''There! Now I have my wand back.''

Jaq and Gus led Cinderella and the fairy godmother back to the kitchen. It was a shambles.

''Anastasia! Drizella! Give me that wand at once!'' Cinderella ordered. ''Haven't you caused enough trouble?''

''Oh, it's you again,'' cackled Drizella. ''Well, now that I know the magic words, I'll put an end to your meddling, once and for all.'' With that, she pointed the wand at Cinderella and the fairy godmother.

''Gus-Gus! We do something 'fore she say that spell,'' squeaked Jaq.

Drizella raised the wand dramatically and began to chant: ''These two are trouble for me and for you . . .''

''I know,'' said Gus. ''Here, Lucifee! Here, kitty, kitty!''

The evil-tempered cat's attention was distracted from the pastry table. With a pleased snarl he bounded after Gus as Drizella continued her spell: ''. . . change them to toads, that's what I'll do . . .''

The two mice raced across the kitchen with the black cat in close pursuit. Gus darted under Drizella's feet just as she was finishing the spell: ''. . . bibbidi-bobbidi-BOO!''

Lucifer crashed into Drizella, causing her to tumble backwards. Everyone watched as the wand flew through the air and came to rest in the hands of the fairy godmother. But it was now pointing right at Cinderella's stepsisters!

In a wink, they were transformed into two warty green toads.

''This is all your fault,'' croaked Anastasia. ''I never should have listened to you.''

The confusion caused Lucifer to stop in his tracks. When he saw the two toads, he forgot all about Jaq and Gus, and chased the two toads right out of the kitchen.

''Godmother!'' cried Cinderella. ''You must change them back before Lucifer catches them.''

''Don't worry,'' chuckled the fairy godmother. ''Lucifer has grown so fat on castle cream that he can't catch anything. I'll reverse the spell, but not until those two have learned their lesson about selfishness—and about stealing magic wands!''

THE WINTER OLYMPICS

The Games of the XIII Winter Olympiad were held in Lake Placid, New York, from February 12 to February 24. More than 1,200 competitors from 37 countries sledded, skated, and skied against the backdrop of the scenic Adirondack Mountains.

Athletes from the Soviet Union returned home from the Winter Games with the most gold medals—10. But it was the United States that presented the most spectacular individual performer—speed skater Eric Heiden—and the most astonishing result—a gold medal for its hockey team.

▶ A SPECTACULAR PERFORMER

Heiden and the hockey team accounted for the 6 gold medals won by the United States in the 38 events. Five of them were captured by Heiden. The 21-year-old from Wisconsin won all the men's speed-skating events—500, 1,000, 1,500, 5,000, and 10,000 meters. He established new Olympic records for all five distances. And in his final assault on the clock, he shattered the world record for 10,000 meters.

No other athlete had ever collected as many as 5 gold medals in a single Winter Olympics. From an individual standpoint, Heiden even surpassed the efforts of swimmer Mark Spitz in the 1972 Summer Olympics. Spitz won 7 gold medals, but only 4 in individual events. He earned the others as a member of relay teams.

▶ A SPECTACULAR VICTORY

On their way to the winners' stand, the U.S. hockey players won 6 games and tied 1. Before the Olympics, no one could have guessed that they would do so well. In an exhibition match prior to the Games, the Soviet team had thrashed them by a score of 10–3.

But when the Games began, the Americans showed their talent with a 7–3 upset over a powerful Czech squad. By the time they met the Soviets, the U.S. record had reached 4 wins, 0 losses, and 1 tie. Recent history, however, weighed heavily against the U.S. team. Soviet hockey teams had won four successive Olympic golds since the U.S. triumph at Squaw Valley, California, in 1960.

With millions watching on television, the

Eric Heiden won all five men's speed-skating events, and he set a new world record in the process.

Goalie Jim Craig blocks a shot in the U.S.–Soviet hockey game, which the Americans won, 4–3.

Americans fought a desperate battle on the way to their 4–3 victory. They fell behind, 2–1, and then 3–2. Each time, Mark Johnson hammered the puck into the Soviet net for the goal that tied the score. In the final period, captain Mike Eruzione scored the winning goal.

As the final day of the tournament began, it was still possible for any of four teams—the United States, Finland, Sweden, or the Soviet Union—to win the gold medal. The United States faced Finland. Again the Americans started sluggishly. They trailed 2–1 after two of the three periods. But Phil Verchota, Rob McClanahan, and Johnson scored in the third period for a 4–2 decision. This victory clinched the gold medal for the United States. In the other final-round game the Soviet Union defeated Sweden, 9–2, for the silver medal.

Throughout the tournament, Jim Craig tended goal brilliantly for the Americans. Much credit was also given to Coach Herb Brooks, who trained his enthusiastic players hard and spurred them on to ever-improving performances.

▶ OTHER WINTER WINNERS

Alpine skiing is a major part of the Winter Games, and the downhill is the glamour event. Austrians captured both the men's and the women's races. Leonhard Stock and Annemarie Moser-Proell outsped their opponents down a steep Whiteface Mountain course. Ingemar Stenmark of Sweden won gold medals in the men's slalom and giant slalom. Hanni Wenzel of tiny Liechtenstein won golds in the women's slalom and giant slalom. She also picked up a silver medal in the downhill.

The Soviets won 4 of their 10 gold medals in Nordic skiing. Nikolai Zimyatov captured 2 individually, in the 30- and 50-kilometer cross-country events. Then he picked up a third as anchorman on the winning 40-kilometer relay team. Ulrich Wehling of East Germany became the first male athlete to win gold medals in the same individual event in three different Olympic Winter Games. In 1972, 1976, and again in 1980, he took first place in the Nordic combined.

Women's figure skating had been something of a special preserve for Americans. Four Americans had won gold medals in the last six Olympics: Tenley Albright (1956), Carol Heiss (1960), Peggy Fleming (1968), and Dorothy Hamill (1976). But in 1980, the top U.S. competitor, Linda Fratianne, was beaten by East Germany's Anett Poetzsch by the slimmest of margins. The final scoring by the judges was 189.00 points for Poetzsch and 188.30 for Fratianne.

In a dazzling performance, Robin Cousins of Britain won the men's figure skating com-

Figure skater Anett Poetzsch of East Germany skated to the gold medal in the women's singles event.

petition. And the Soviet Union's Irina Rodnina and Alexander Zaitsev repeated their 1976 Olympic triumph in the pairs figure skating. The highly regarded U.S. combination of Tai Babilonia and Randy Gardner, who had won the 1979 world championship, was forced to withdraw because of an injury to Gardner.

Meinhard Nehmer of East Germany won a gold medal in the bobsled competition for the second Olympics in a row. He piloted the four-man sled down the Mount Van Hoevenberg course in record times. Two of the team's four runs were under one minute, the fastest in Olympic history. In the two-man bobsled event, the Swiss team took the gold.

In the luge competition, East Germany dominated the men's events. Bernhard Glass won the singles. The team of Hans Rinn and Norbert Hahn repeated their gold-medal performance of 1976. The women's singles was won by Vera Zozulya of the Soviet Union.

Among the nations that sent their athletes to Lake Placid, the Soviet Union, East Germany, and the United States were the principal collectors of medals. The Russians accumulated the most gold, but the East Germans actually exceeded them in total medals with 23—9 gold, 7 silver, and 7 bronze. The Russians had 22, adding 6 silver and 6 bronze to their 10 gold. The United States totaled 12, with 4 silver and 2 bronze in addition to the 6 gold.

Aside from five-time winner Heiden, silver medalist Fratianne, and the hockey team, the U.S. medalists were: Leah Poulos Mueller, 2 silver, in the women's 500- and 1,000-meter speed skating; Phil Mahre, a silver in the men's slalom; Beth Heiden, a bronze in the women's 3,000-meter speed skating; and Charles Tickner, a bronze in the men's figure skating.

Canadian Olympians won two medals at Lake Placid. Gaetan Boucher of Quebec won a silver in the men's 1,000-meter speed skating. Stephen Podborski of Ontario took the bronze in the men's downhill skiing.

For the United States, the total of 12 medals was the country's best showing at a Winter Olympics since 1952. While this was outstanding, Americans will best remember the 1980 Winter Games for Eric Heiden and the spunky young hockey squad.

Austrian Leonhard Stock outskied all his opponents in the men's downhill.

FINAL MEDAL STANDINGS

Winter Games—Lake Placid, New York

Country	Gold	Silver	Bronze	Total
Soviet Union	10	6	6	22
East Germany	9	7	7	23
United States	6	4	2	12
Austria	3	2	2	7
Sweden	3	0	1	4
Liechtenstein	2	2	0	4
Finland	1	5	3	9
Norway	1	3	6	10
Netherlands	1	2	1	4
Switzerland	1	1	3	5
Britain	1	0	0	1
West Germany	0	2	3	5
Italy	0	2	0	2
Canada	0	1	1	2
Hungary	0	1	0	1
Japan	0	1	0	1
Bulgaria	0	0	1	1
Czechoslovakia	0	0	1	1
France	0	0	1	1

ERIC HEIDEN, OLYMPIC HERO

A flashing smile . . . great enthusiasm . . . good humored . . . intense and hard working. These are some of the phrases that have been used to describe Eric Heiden, the Olympic hero of the 1980 Winter Games. The 21-year-old premed student from Madison, Wisconsin, captured the attention and the hearts of the American public when he won all five gold medals for speed skating at Lake Placid, New York. That was the largest number of golds ever attained by one athlete in the Winter Games.

Although Heiden was internationally well known prior to the Olympics, his rise to fame went almost unnoticed by the American public when it began back in 1977. The cause was a lack of interest on the part of Americans in the sport of speed skating—except in the Great Lakes region, Heiden's home base. So when Heiden won the 1977 men's world speed-skating championship at Heerenveen, the Netherlands, not too many Americans paid attention. And they seemed just as unaware when he captured the same title two more times, in 1978 and 1979. The lack of fuss was fine with Heiden, who after becoming an American idol said, "I really liked it best when I was a nobody."

Eric and his younger sister, Beth, an Olympic bronze medalist in speed skating, have never had star complexes. Excellence in sports has always been a natural way of life for them. They were both raised in a down-to-earth, sports-loving home with a gym in the basement. Grandfather Art Thomsen, a former ice hockey coach at the University of Wisconsin, led both Eric and Beth out onto the ice as children. Then he watched over them as they developed into good skaters.

It was Beth who first became interested in speed skating. Then Eric joined her in practice sessions at her speed-skating club. This is where coach Dianne Holum spotted the Heidens and started grooming them for big-time competition. Besides natural talent, both youngsters had two other traits that help make champions. They were very hard workers and had lots of stick-to-itiveness.

That these traits remained with Eric is shown in a story told by Peter Schotting, who coached the U.S. men's speed-skating team at the Lake Placid Olympics. Schotting would sometimes give the team the afternoon off. But he said he always knew there would be one lone figure still working out after the others had gone. That lone figure, always refusing to rest, always striving to keep his body in condition, was Eric Heiden.

As the 1980 speed-skating season was drawing to an end, it appeared that Heiden was thinking of putting his abilities into other sports. He told reporters that he was going to quit competitive skating and turn to bicycle racing and hockey. He also wanted to complete his university studies, specializing in sports medicine.

THE SUMMER OLYMPICS

The Summer Games of the XXII Olympiad were held in Moscow, U.S.S.R., from July 19 to August 3. Nearly 6,000 athletes from 81 countries participated in the program, which included 22 sports. But more than 50 nations refused to take part in the Games, supporting a United States-led boycott. The boycott was in response to the Soviet Union's invasion of Afghanistan, in 1979. There were also mild forms of protest from some of those countries that did take part.

Because of the absence of so many competitors, the Soviet team reaped an even larger medal harvest than usual. Soviet athletes won 197 medals, including 80 golds. These totals surpassed the Soviets' previous best Olympic achievements—125 total medals in 1976, and 50 golds in 1972.

East Germany finished second in total medals, 126, and in golds, 47. Bulgaria was third with 40 medals, 8 of which were gold. Among the non-Communist nations at the Games, Britain was the most successful, with 21 medals, including 5 golds.

Track and Field. Track and field, the showcase sport of the Olympics, attracted 100,000 spectators each day at the Lenin Stadium. The competition produced rich hauls of gold for the Soviets and the East Germans, who collected 15 and 11 victories, respectively. But the glamor events were won by athletes from Britain. The British won four golds, led by rival middle-distance stars Steve Ovett and Sebastian Coe. In a tense head-to-head competition, Ovett beat Coe in the 800-meter run. Later in the week, Coe turned the tables on Ovett with a spectacular finish in the 1,500.

The other British victors were Daley Thompson in the two-day, ten-event decathlon, and Allan Wells, a Scot, in the 100-meter dash. Wells was foiled in his bid to win the "sprint double" when Pietro Mennea of Italy nipped him at the tape in the 200-meter race.

Miruts Yifter of Ethiopia won the "distance double"—the 5,000- and the 10,000-meter runs. He ended the reign of Finland's Lasse Viren, who had won both races in each of the two previous Olympics.

World record breakers included East Ger-

Britain's runners were led by rival stars Steve Ovett (279) and Sebastian Coe (254). They each won a gold.

Miruts Yifter (191) of Ethiopia won the "distance double"—the 5,000-meter and 10,000-meter runs.

85

many's Gerd Wessig in the high jump, Poland's Wladyslaw Kozakiewicz in the pole vault, and Yuri Sedykh of the Soviet Union in the hammer throw. There was also a remarkable effort by long-jump winner Lutz Dombrowski. The East German sailed 28 feet, ¼ inch (8.5 meters), the second best leap in history.

Waldemar Cierpinski of East Germany won his second consecutive Olympic marathon. The only other runner to win two Olympic marathons was Abebe Bikila of Ethiopia, who won in 1960 and 1964.

In the women's competition, Nadyezhda Olizarenko of the Soviet Union took the gold medal in the 800-meter run with a world record time. Her teammate, Tatyana Kazankina, set an Olympic record in winning the 1,500. Kazankina had won both the 800 and the 1,500 at the Montreal Olympics in 1976. Baerbel Eckert Wockel of East Germany bettered her own Olympic record in the 200-meter dash, which she won for the second straight time.

Swimming. The swimming competition, too, produced some excellent performances. Men swimmers of the Soviet Union had failed to win a gold medal in the 1976 Olympics at Montreal, but in their homeland they reached the victor's podium seven times. The absence of the American men may have contributed to the Soviet success. But at least one of the Soviet athletes, Vladimir Salnikov, might very well have been unbeatable even if the Americans had competed.

Salnikov, a 20-year-old student, captured gold medals in the 400-meter and 1,500-meter freestyle events, and as a member of the 800-meter freestyle relay team. In the 1,500, he set a world record of 14:58.27, becoming the first swimmer in history to cover the distance in less than 15 minutes. In the 400-meter, he set an Olympic record.

Duncan Goodhew won Britain's only gold medal in swimming, in the 100-meter breaststroke event.

The East German women were as dominant in the pool as they had been four years

Soviet swimmer Vladimir Salnikov captured gold medals in the 400-meter and 1,500-meter freestyle events, and as a member of the 800-meter freestyle relay team.

Soviet gymnast Nelli Kim (right) tied with Nadia Comaneci for the gold medal in the floor exercises.

earlier. In Montreal, they had won gold medals in 11 of the 13 events, and they duplicated that effort in Moscow. Three of the East German women—Rica Reinisch, Barbara Krause, and Caren Metschuck—won three gold medals apiece. Reinisch, a 15-year-old student, shattered world records in winning the 100-meter backstroke and the 200-meter backstroke. She was also a member of the winning medley relay team. Krause captured the 100- and 200-meter freestyle events, and she, too, was on the medley relay team. Metschuck was the 100-meter butterfly victor, and she contributed to two relay triumphs.

Gymnastics. The darling of the 1976 Olympics had been 14-year-old Nadia Comaneci, the Rumanian gymnast. In the 1980 Games, Comaneci tried to repeat her gold-medal victory in the all-around competition. But she had to settle for a silver, as Yelena Davydova of the Soviet Union took the gold. Comaneci did win a gold on the balance beam, and she and Nelli Kim of the Soviet Union tied for the gold in the floor exercises.

In the men's events, Soviet gymnast Alexander Dityatin was the big star. He emerged as the Games' most prolific medal winner: three golds, four silvers, and one bronze.

The Soviet Union won the team titles in both the women's and men's divisions.

Other Events. Boxing, dominated by the United States four years earlier, became almost an all-Cuban show. Of the 11 weight classes, the Cubans won 6 of the gold medals. Cuban heavyweight Teofilo Stevenson repeated his gold medal triumphs of 1972 and 1976. Only one other Olympic boxer, Laszlo Papp of Hungary, has ever won three golds.

In men's basketball, Yugoslavia won the gold medal by defeating Italy. Both teams had beaten the Soviets in early games, and the host team had to settle for the bronze. But in the women's competition, the Soviets took the gold.

In soccer, the Czechs dethroned the defending Olympic champion, East Germany.

Alexander Dityatin, another gymnast from the Soviet Union, won the most medals at the Summer Games: three golds, four silvers, and one bronze.

FINAL MEDAL STANDINGS

Summer Games—Moscow, U.S.S.R.

Country	Gold	Silver	Bronze	Total
U.S.S.R.	80	70	47	197
East Germany	47	36	43	126
Bulgaria	8	16	16	40
Cuba	8	7	5	20
Italy	8	3	4	15
Hungary	7	10	15	32
Rumania	6	6	13	25
France	6	5	3	14
Britain	5	7	9	21
Poland	3	14	14	31
Sweden	3	3	6	12
Finland	3	1	4	8
Yugoslavia	2	3	4	9
Czechoslovakia	2	2	9	13
Australia	2	2	5	9
Denmark	2	1	2	5
Brazil	2	0	2	4
Ethiopia	2	0	2	4
Switzerland	2	0	0	2
Spain	1	3	2	6
Austria	1	3	1	5
Greece	1	0	2	3
Belgium	1	0	0	1
India	1	0	0	1
Venezuela	1	0	0	1
Zimbabwe	1	0	0	1
North Korea	0	3	2	5
Mongolia	0	2	2	4
Tanzania	0	2	0	2
Mexico	0	1	3	4
Netherlands	0	1	3	4
Ireland	0	1	1	2
Uganda	0	1	0	1
Jamaica	0	0	3	3
Guyana	0	0	1	1
Lebanon	0	0	1	1

BOX ART

Here is an easy way to change an ordinary box into one that is pretty—and pretty unusual. The boxes can be used to hold jewelry, paper clips, or any of your favorite small treasures. You can also fill them with candy or small gifts and give them to friends.

Each box will be your own unique creation. You can work with tiny candies, macaroni, dried peas, sunflower seeds, coffee beans—the list of dry foods you can use is long and varied. On a red box, use alphabet pasta to create a message such as "I think you're nice." Paint a box bright blue. Then glue on a snowman made of rice, with peppercorns for the eyes and a red-painted grain of rice for the mouth. Make a tulip using lentils and bay leaves, on a white box.

All you have to do is (1) decide on your design, (2) select the foods you wish to use, (3) choose or paint a box in a complimentary color, (4) arrange the design on the box cover, and (5) glue each piece down.

To prevent the decorations from attracting insects, and to keep the decorations from coming loose, you should seal the surface. Try a water-based sealer or an acrylic spray, both of which are available at art and craft supply stores. Or use clear nail polish. Cover the entire top of the box with the sealer. Be sure to cover the sides and the top of every piece of food. Apply several coats of the sealer. Let each coat dry thoroughly before you apply the next coat.

KING TUT

New Beginning, by Shelly Stoft, 17, Reseda, California

YOUNG PHOTOGRAPHERS

On these pages, ghostly flowers sprout from a weathered house. A tiger changes its stripes. Fire-red berries are locked in ice and a tree is transformed by geometry. These images, like the others shown here, share one striking quality—all were planned and photographed with painstaking care.

The photographs have something else in common, too. They were winners in the 1980 Scholastic/Kodak Photo Awards program, which was open to junior and senior high school students in the United States and Canada. What advice do the winning young photographers have for others? Make your photographs interesting. Be patient when you take them. And practice until you can take a perfect picture.

Diamond Shapes,
by Bill Wood, 16, South Bend, Indiana

Teardrops from Heaven, by Devin Lushbaugh, 15, High Point, North Carolina

Colorful Tiger, by Joni Dwyer, 18, Aurora, Colorado

Desert Inn,
by Perry Kuklin, 17, Reseda, California

Untitled, by Kathy Kovacs, 17, Aurora, Colorado

NETSUKE—MINIATURE SCULPTURES

The carvings you see on these pages are called netsuke (NET-skay). Most of them are small enough to fit into the palm of your hand. They were made in Japan by master carvers, mostly in the 18th and 19th centuries. Some netsuke have very intricate designs, and so it is not surprising that a carver sometimes needed two or three months to make a single netsuke.

Today many netsuke are recognized as fine works of art. But they weren't originally made as works of art. They had an ordinary, everyday function—much as jewelry and furniture have everyday functions.

Nowadays most Japanese people wear the same kinds of clothes worn by people in North America. But this has not always been true. The traditional Japanese outfit was a loose robe called a kimono. Around the waist of the kimono was a sash called an obi. The kimono had no pockets. How, then, could Japanese people carry small objects such as money and pipe tobacco?

This problem was solved by putting the objects into small containers. A cord was threaded through small holes in the container, and a netsuke was attached to the free end of the cord. The netsuke rested on the upper edge of the obi, serving as a counterweight for the container, which hung down below the obi. Both netsuke and container enhanced the beauty of the kimono.

No one is certain when netsuke were first used. The earliest ones were quite simple in design, and there was not much demand for them. But by the late 1700's, so many people wanted these small objects that hundreds of carvers did nothing but carve netsuke.

Most netsuke are made of ivory or wood. But other materials have also been used, including bone, horn, shell, amber, stone, metal, and porcelain. Although each netsuke is unique, all netsuke do have some characteristics in common. They are smooth. There are no sharp edges that could tear the kimono. Each netsuke has two small holes through which the cord can pass. These holes are often cleverly worked into the design, so that they are difficult to see.

Among the most popular subjects for netsuke are animals. Some of the animals are easily recognized—monkeys, horses, rats, dogs, tigers, snakes, fish, even insects and snails. Other animals derive from mythology or legend, such as the shishi, the shokuin, and the kappa. The shishi is a curly-haired cross between a dog and a lion. It is a symbol of strength and courage. Male shishis are often shown with open mouths. Female shishis usually have closed mouths.

This netsuke illustrates the legend of Chōkwarō.

Plum blossoms are popular netsuke subjects.

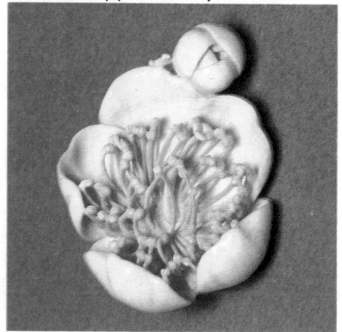

The shokuin is a dragonlike beast. It has the head of a man and the body of a snake. It is believed to control the changing of the seasons.

The kappa was an imaginary creature that lived in rivers. He is usually shown having the head of a monkey, the body of a tortoise, and webbed feet. Japanese children were often warned to watch out for the kappa. Sometimes children who didn't know how to swim would go into rivers and drown. Their deaths were blamed on the kappa. Many netsuke show the kappa sitting on a turtle, one of his companions in the river. Others show him wearing a turtle shell. Another netsuke shows a kappa clutching a large cucumber. The kappa was believed to love cucumbers, and Japanese people sometimes left cucumbers beside river banks. They hoped these offerings would please the kappa, so that the kappa wouldn't bother them.

One beautiful ivory netsuke shows a horse coming out of a gourd. It refers to the legend of Chōkwarō, a Chinese religious figure who was believed to have lived around the end of the 7th century. According to legend, he had a white horse that could carry him thousands of miles in a single day. When his trip was finished, Chokwarō would put the horse in a small gourd. When he wanted to ride the horse again, all he had to do was wet the gourd and the horse would come out.

Another netsuke subject is Ono no Koma-

This dragonlike creature is a shokuin.

chi, a famous poet who lived in the 9th century. Some netsuke show Komachi when she was young and beautiful. Others show her when she was old and no longer attractive. They make us think of some of her poetry:

> The cherry blossoms
> Have passed away, their color lost,
>   While to no avail
> Age takes my beauty as it falls
> In the long rain of my regret.

The delicate flowers of cherry, plum, and other plants are also popular subjects of netsuke carvers. So is the chrysanthemum, which is one of the favorite flowers of the Japanese people.

Today netsuke are collected by people all over the world. Many are worth more than their weight in gold. A netsuke of good quality costs from several hundred dollars to more than $20,000. And the value keeps going up.

Master carvers in Japan are still making netsuke. People seldom wear kimonos, but they still buy netsuke because the tiny sculptures are so very beautiful to look at.

Reviewed by MARY GARDNER NEILL
Curator of Oriental Art
Yale University Art Gallery

The kappa was an imaginary river creature.

ELEGANT EGGS

Sometimes the most beautiful crafts are the easiest to make. These lovely eggs are a perfect example. They are made of sugar, icing, and bits of jewelry. But the most important ingredient is your imagination. The eggs make wonderful gifts. And they are long-lasting gifts, too. If kept safe and dry, they will last for years.

WHAT TO USE

Sugar
Egg white
Food coloring (optional)
Plastic egg mold
Decorating tube with 10-inch (25-centimeter) bag and small star tip
Confectioners' powdered sugar
Cream of tartar
Bits of broken jewelry, sequins, glitter, gold thread

HOW TO MAKE THE EGG

1. Use about 1 cup of sugar for each egg. Dampen the sugar with the egg white and mix well. The mixture should have the consistency of wet sand. You can make a colored egg by adding a drop or two of food coloring to this mixture.

2. Take the mold for half the egg. Press the damp sugar firmly into the mold.

3. Turn the mold over onto a cookie sheet or a piece of aluminum foil. Gently remove the mold.

4. Repeat steps 2 and 3 using the second half of the mold.

5. Let the sugar dry for about a half hour.

6. Using a teaspoon, scoop out the center of each sugar mold. This must be done very carefully. Hollow out the center until you have a shell that is about ¼ inch (.6 centimeter) thick. (The sugar you remove can be used to make another egg.)

7. Let the egg halves dry overnight.

HOW TO DECORATE THE EGG

1. Prepare the icing. Use about 1 cup of confectioners' sugar for each egg. Add enough water to the sugar to form a smooth paste. Add ¼ teaspoon of cream of tartar to the mixture.

2. Use some of the icing to cement together the two halves of the egg.

3. Let the egg dry for at least three hours. Put the left-over icing in a closed container. Refrigerate the icing until you are ready for step 4.

4. Fill the bag of the decorating tube with icing. Cover the seam where the two egg halves meet with little star-shaped flowers. Also decorate the top of the egg with star-shaped flowers.

5. Finish decorating the egg with pieces of jewelry or other pretty objects. Gently press the pieces into the icing.

6. Let the finished egg dry overnight.

FABULOUS FABERGÉ

The most fabulous eggs ever made were created by Peter Carl Fabergé. Fabergé was a Russian goldsmith and designer who lived from 1846 to 1920. He designed many jeweled items for the rulers of Russia. But he was most famous for his eggs. The eggs were made of enameled metal and were decorated with gold and beautiful jewels. Many of Fabergé's eggs were actually little boxes that could be opened. One of these eggs contained a tiny model of a Russian palace.

PINOCCHIO GOES TO SEA

Geppetto looked down at Pinocchio's report card. Pinocchio looked down at his shoes. It wasn't a very good report.

"Pinocchio, you must spend more time studying," said Geppetto, wagging a finger at the little puppet. "You'll never grow up to be a shopkeeper or a wood-carver if you can't read or add."

"I don't want to be a shopkeeper," argued Pinocchio. "I want to be a sailor, like the ones in the book you've been reading to me."

Geppetto was worried. How could he get Pinocchio to study? Then he had an idea. "That's just the trouble, you little wooden-head," sighed Geppetto. "I guess I've been distracting you from your studies. I won't read to you anymore from *Treasure Island* until your grades improve."

Pinocchio went to his room to study, but he couldn't keep his mind on math problems. Instead, he thought of *Treasure Island* and sailing the high seas.

When Geppetto came to Pinocchio's room that night, he found the little puppet fast asleep, his math homework still unsolved.

Geppetto gently pulled the covers up around Pinocchio's neck and tiptoed out of the room.

"Perhaps he'll do better tomorrow," he thought.

The morning star was just beginning to fade when Pinocchio woke up with a start. "Hey, Jiminy!" he cried.

The cricket sat up in his matchbox-bed and rubbed his eyes. "What's the matter, Pinocchio?"

"I've just had a wonderful dream. We were sailors, and we found Treasure Island. There were jewels hanging from the trees and gold heaped everywhere."

"It was only a dream," yawned Jiminy. "Go back to sleep."

Pinocchio paid no attention. He jumped from his bed and began opening drawers and stuffing clothes into his pillowcase. "Come on, Jiminy," he laughed, "we're going to sea!"

There was nothing Jiminy could do but follow.

It was daylight when they reached the harbor. Anchored at the end of the dock was a three-masted ship. To Pinocchio it looked just like the ship in *Treasure Island*. He could see the crew climbing the masts and preparing to set sail.

"What luck," cried Pinocchio. "She's sailing with the morning tide."

He ran down the dock toward a tall man in a black coat, who was standing at the gangplank shouting orders.

"I want to become a member of your crew," blurted Pinocchio.

The captain looked down at the small boy. "Can you read a map or a compass? Can you calculate a position by the Pole Star? Have you studied ships' rigging?"

Pinocchio was about to answer, "Yes." Then he remembered what had happened to his nose the last time he had lied.

"No," confessed the puppet.

"Can you write well enough to keep the ship's log?" asked the captain.

"Not that well," admitted Pinocchio.

The captain frowned at the eager puppet. "If you can't read or write or figure, there's only one job for you, and it just so happens it's open. Follow me."

The tall captain led Pinocchio up the gangplank and ordered the ship to set sail. Sailors scurried off to haul up the anchor and cast off the lines. No one noticed that a small, green cricket had hopped aboard.

Pinocchio followed the captain below deck to the galley, where he was introduced to the ship's cook as "his new helper."

The cook was a short, red-faced man who huffed and puffed as he hurried around the kitchen snapping orders at Pinocchio.

"That pan there! Pots over here! Not there, woodenhead, over here!"

When the gear had been stowed, the cook sat Pinocchio down in front of a big sack of potatoes and handed him a knife.

"Peel," he ordered.

"All of them?" Pinocchio asked, looking at the huge pile of potatoes in front of him.

"All of them," snapped the cook. "There's more where those came from, and pots to wash and the deck to scrub."

Three days later, Pinocchio's arms hurt and his back ached. But he had to keep on peeling. "Not my idea of adventure," he grumbled. He'd been three days at sea, and all he'd seen were potatoes and pans.

Pinocchio had nearly finished the afternoon potatoes when the cries and cheers of the sailors on deck made him drop his knife and run topside.

One of the men had netted a large sea turtle and was hoisting it aboard while the crew applauded.

"Turtle soup for dinner, lads," yelled the

cook, who was leaning over the ship's rail, rubbing his fat hands together. "I'll be back with me knives."

The sailors flipped the turtle onto its back. As they watched its struggles, they eagerly anticipated a meal of something besides fish.

Pinocchio watched the turtle wave its legs wildly in the air as it struggled to turn over. "You're trapped on this ship, too," he thought. The turtle had stopped thrashing and was now looking at him with big, sad eyes.

The rest of the crew was so distracted by the thought of piping hot turtle soup that the captain's roar of "Avast!" took them by surprise. "Batten the hatches! Man the shrouds!" the captain cried, and the crew scrambled to obey. A sudden storm was brewing, and the turtle was temporarily forgotten in the rush to secure the ship.

But Pinocchio hadn't forgotten about the turtle. He felt sorry for the poor creature, and he took advantage of the confusion to push it across the deck. Its shell scraped along as Pinocchio inched the turtle over to the gangway opening. He gave one last mighty shove, and the turtle went over the side to land in the water with a splash. As Pinocchio watched the turtle swim away, the deck began to pitch.

"Quick! We'll be safe here," called a small, familiar voice. Pinocchio looked around to see Jiminy Cricket perched on the lip of an empty barrel.

"In here," Jiminy called, and Pinocchio climbed inside. The two friends huddled at the bottom of the barrel.

The sky grew black, and the ship pitched wildly. Lightning flashed, and rain poured into the barrel, drenching the shivering pair.

The deck heaved. Thunder boomed. A huge wave crashed down on the ship and swept the barrel over the side.

Pinocchio and Jiminy held their breath as they sailed through the air and splashed into the rough sea. Luck was with them, though, for the barrel landed right side up.

"Boy overboard!" shouted Pinocchio, but his voice was carried away by the raging storm. "Why, oh why did I ever want to be a sailor?" moaned the puppet as he and Jiminy helplessly watched the ship disappear into the dark.

They spent a wet night in the open barrel, bobbing up and down in the swells. But by morning the storm had broken, leaving them floating on a calm sea, with no land in sight.

"I wish I were anywhere but here," wailed Pinocchio. "Even in school. If I ever get back to land, I'll do my homework every night and study hard, so I can be a good shopkeeper when I grow up!"

Jiminy tried to cheer him up. "There's bound to be another ship along in a couple of days," he said.

Just then they felt something bump the barrel.

"What was that?" said Jiminy from the bottom of the barrel, hoping it wasn't a hungry fish.

Pinocchio peered over the top. There was a bright green head peeking out from beneath a broad green shell.

"It's a sea turtle," said Pinocchio. He held Jiminy up so he could see.

"Look," said the cricket, pointing to the scrape marks on the turtle's shell. "It's the same one you saved from the cook. Now he's come to save us."

They quickly climbed onto the turtle's back. And soon they were safely on shore, watching the turtle swim back to sea.

When Pinocchio and Jiminy finally reached Geppetto's woodcarving shop, waterlogged but safe, they were welcomed with tears, hugs, and a mild scolding.

Much to Geppetto's surprise, Pinocchio's grades soon began to improve. He even got a prize for turning in the most book reports.

There was one funny thing, though: Geppetto never could figure out why the little puppet never wrote a book report on *Treasure Island*.

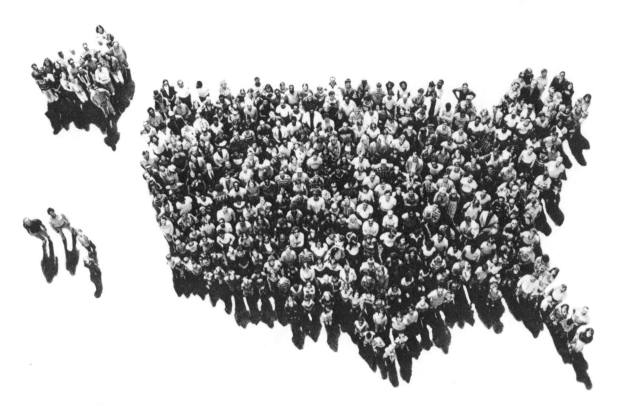

THE COUNTING OF AMERICA

Chances are that you and each member of your family went down in history on April 1, 1980—as part of the biggest head count ever undertaken in the United States. The count was the U.S. Government's twentieth census of population and housing. It tried to reach everyone living in the country, more than 220,000,000 people.

Questionnaires were mailed to over 80,000,000 households. Laid end to end, the forms easily would have circled the earth. In all, they asked for some 3,300,000,000 (billion) items of information. What did the government want to know? Beyond mere numbers, the 1980 census was designed to provide a detailed picture of the United States—who its people are, where they're from, and where and how they live and work.

▶ REASONS BEHIND THE CENSUS

The original purpose of the U.S. census was to ensure that everyone is properly represented in the House of Representatives. The Constitution guarantees each state at least one seat in the House. The rest of the 435 seats are divided up among the states on the basis of their populations, using decennial (taken every ten years) census figures.

Every ten years, the seats are reapportioned, or divided up again, to reflect changes in population.

Census figures are also used to draw the boundaries of Congressional voting districts, so that each district will have roughly the same number of people as the next. This helps guarantee that everyone is represented equally in Congress. And state and local governments use the census figures to redraw their own legislative districts.

Other information gotten through the census, along with population figures, helps determine how billions of dollars in federal funds will be used each year. More than 100 federal programs use census information to find out which areas are most in need of funds. These programs range from aid for highway construction to school lunch and reading development programs.

Towns, civic groups, businesses, and individuals use the figures, too. For example, figures showing the number of preschool children in your town could help the town decide if a new school will be needed. And census figures help businesses know where to build new stores for potential shoppers, and new manufacturing plants for potential workers.

▶ HOW THE CENSUS WAS TAKEN

Most households received a basic questionnaire that took about fifteen minutes to fill out. Some households were asked more detailed questions on a longer form. Most households were instructed to simply mail the form back to a district office of the Census Bureau. But for others, census workers went out to get the forms. Many of these households were in areas where few people live and where mail delivery is sometimes difficult. This meant that the census workers sometimes had to travel up mountain trails or across rough country by jeep or even on horseback.

Census workers also counted people in jails, and hotels, checked in all-night movie theaters and taverns, and went looking for illegal immigrants and others who might have been overlooked when the questionnaires were mailed out. They looked, too, for people who simply hadn't replied to the census.

By law, everyone must answer the census, and the Census Bureau must keep the answers confidential. But some people thought the government's questions were too personal or were afraid the information would be used against them in some way. This problem was greatest in cities and among minority groups. The Census Bureau estimated that in the 1970 census it had undercounted the total population by 2.5 percent but had undercounted blacks by 7.7 percent.

In 1980, the bureau tried to offset the "undercount" by working with minority group leaders. It launched an advertising campaign, with the slogan "We're counting on you." And it developed special programs for schools, in the hope that children would convince their parents to fill out the forms.

▶ ADDING IT UP

By June, most of the forms had been returned to district offices. Census workers checked them over and then shipped them to one of three processing centers, in Indiana, Louisiana, and California. There, high-speed cameras photographed the forms on microfilm. The microfilm was scanned by an electronic device, and the answers were transmitted with lightning speed to a computer system in Maryland.

The computers whirred around the clock to sort and add the answers. The Census Bureau released some figures in late summer. About 300,000 pages of detailed reports would follow.

The early figures were controversial. Some people said that the results should not be used to apportion seats in Congress because aliens had been counted. And when the figures showed sharp declines in population for many older cities, the cities charged that the census had not been taken carefully. Some cities—and some minority groups—wanted the figures adjusted or recounted. A

More than 80,000,000 households were asked to fill out census questionnaires.

few cities took their cases to court. But census officials said that, even allowing for an undercount, the cities' populations had in fact declined. Some areas seemed certain to lose federal funds and representation in Congress, even if recounts were taken.

▶ HISTORY OF THE CENSUS

The Constitution provided for the first census and for those that followed every ten years. The first census, in 1790, was directed by Thomas Jefferson, who was then secretary of state. He delegated the job to the U.S. marshals, who in turn hired assistants. The census takers fanned out over the thirteen existing states, traveling by foot, horseback, or boat. Travel wasn't easy—roads and bridges were few. It took six days to go from New York to Boston, a trip that takes 40 minutes by jet today.

The census takers asked just six questions: the name of the household head and the numbers of free white males aged 16 or older, free white males under 16, free white females, other free persons, and slaves. No forms were provided, so the census takers jotted the replies on whatever paper was handy. Results, with names, were posted in each town and village. People who hadn't been counted were supposed to add their names to the list. The count showed a population of just under 4,000,000. But many people had avoided the census takers, and others had simply been missed. Jefferson himself had to add his name to the list in Philadelphia.

As the country grew in the 1800's, census takers faced a bigger and bigger job. Printed census forms came into use in 1830. And by 1860, there were six separate questionnaires, with 142 questions. The answers were added by hand, and there were many errors. By 1880, there were 50,000,000 people living in 38 states and 9 territories. Congress set up a census office, which was deluged with data. It was still publishing results in 1887. Then, in time for the 1890 census, a new method of mechanical tabulation was developed. It relied on punch cards, and it revolutionized information processing.

Some of the biggest changes in the census took place in the 20th century. In 1902, the census office became a bureau of the Department of Commerce. The bureau first experimented with mailed forms in 1910, and in 1940 it used scientific sampling for the first time. (Scientific sampling is a way of getting a picture of the whole population by questioning a small number of households.) During World War II, census information was used in hundreds of special surveys of manpower and industrial resources. After the

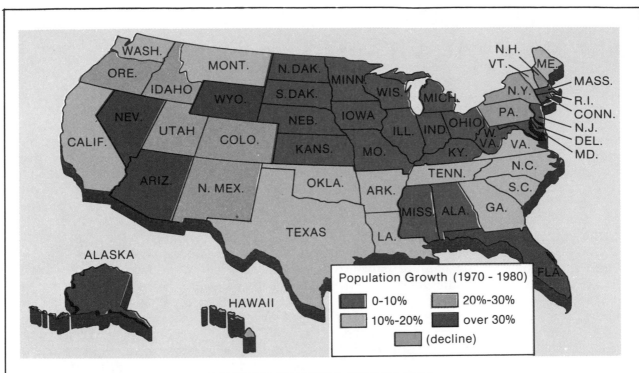

Population Growth (1970 - 1980)

- 0-10%
- 10%-20%
- 20%-30%
- over 30%
- (decline)

LOOKING THROUGH A CRYSTAL BALL

Long before the first questionnaires were mailed out, census officials had been predicting what the 1980 count would show. They were able to do this because each month the Census Bureau surveys about 50,000 households. The results of these surveys give the bureau a sort of crystal ball, through which it can keep abreast of changes in housing and population.

Based on the monthly counts, here are some of the trends that the 1980 census was expected to show:

• People have been leaving the Northeast and moving to southern and western states. This trend would affect seats in the House of Representatives. States that gained population would gain seats—and with them, a stronger voice in the federal government.

• The total U.S. population in 1980 was slightly more than 222,000,000, up about 9 percent from 1970. This would be the smallest percent for any ten-year period since the 1930's. (The actual total turned out to be closer to 226,000,000.)

• The traditional family of mother, father, and one or more children accounted for less than a third of U.S. households, the lowest proportion ever. And the number of households headed by women rose by nearly 50 percent in the ten years since 1970.

• In about half of the husband-wife families, both partners worked—a new high. But family income rose just 4 percent since 1970, compared with a 34-percent increase in the preceding ten years.

• For only the second time in U.S. history, the average age of the population was over 30. (The first time was in 1950, before the "baby boom" that followed World War II began to affect the statistics.) One result of this trend is that people over 65 will soon outnumber teenagers.

war, the bureau offered similar services to government agencies, universities, and research organizations. Computers, introduced in the 1950's, made more information available faster. And in 1960 and 1970, census taking by mail was used extensively.

For nearly two centuries, the growth of the United States and the changes in the life of its people have been chronicled by the U.S. census. Census figures show that if you had been born in the United States in 1850, you probably would have lived on a farm. You probably would not have graduated from high school—only 2 percent of 18-year-olds had done so in 1870. By contrast, if you were born in 1970, you are mostly likely to live in a city or a suburb. And your chances of finishing high school are 80 percent.

ANIMAL PARTNERSHIPS

Life can be very dangerous for a little fish in a big ocean. Lots of big fish are always eager to eat little fish. One little fish has a good solution to this problem. The fish is the pilotfish. Its solution: it lives with sharks. It is not uncommon to see a shark accompanied by six or more pilotfish. Any big fish foolish enough to chase one of these pilotfish risks the chance of being eaten by the shark.

Don't the sharks eat the pilotfish? No. The sharks also benefit from the relationship. Pilotfish eat some of the harmful parasites that live on the sharks' bodies.

Sharks have a similar relationship with remoras. Remoras are warm-water fish that have powerful suckers on the tops of their heads. They use these suckers to attach themselves to sharks, swordfish, porpoises, and other large sea animals. One kind of remora, the whalesucker, attaches itself to whales.

The remora benefits in several ways. It is protected from enemies. It gets some food. And it gets a free ride to new fishing grounds. The larger animal benefits from the remora's parasite-cleaning activities.

Partnerships between two different kinds of animals are common in nature. The best partnerships are those from which both animals benefit. But there are also partnerships from which only one of the animals appears to benefit. Butterfish often spend the first year of their lives under the umbrella of jellyfish. They gain protection and can feed on the tiny animals that get trapped by the tentacles of the jellyfish. The jellyfish do not seem to get any benefit from the relationship. A jellyfish may occasionally eat one of the butterfish. In general, however, the thick mucus that covers the butterfish seems to protect them from a jellyfish's hunger.

Many crabs form partnerships with other animals. One partnership involves crabs and sponges. The crab—called, appropriately enough, the sponge crab—looks around until it finds the right kind of sponge. The crab detaches the sponge from its resting place and puts it on top of its shell. Small hairlike structures on the crab's shell help hold the sponge. The crab may also use its hind legs to hold the sponge.

As the crab grows bigger, so does the sponge. Eventually, the sponge completely covers the crab's shell, thus hiding the crab

Remoras are small fish that attach themselves to sharks. They are thus protected from enemies, and they get a free ride. The shark benefits from the remora's parasite-cleaning activities.

A sponge crab carries a sponge on the top of its shell. The sponge hides the crab from its enemies. And as the crab moves along the ocean floor, water currents carry food to the sponge.

from enemies (almost no one likes to eat sponges). As the crab moves along the ocean floor, water currents pass around and through the sponge, carrying food particles that the sponge can eat.

Grenadier crabs carry sea anemones in their claws. If an enemy approaches, a grenadier crab stretches out its claws, right into the face of the attacker. Instead of an easy dinner, the attacker must deal with the poisonous tentacles of the anemones.

In addition to providing protection, the anemones sometimes provide the crab with food. But they do not do this willingly. If an anemone catches a small fish with its tentacles, it must quickly push the fish into its mouth. Otherwise, the grenadier crab may steal the fish.

The grenadier crab isn't faithful to its helpful anemones. If it sees an anemone larger than one of those it is carrying, it will drop the anemone in its claw and pick up the larger one.

▶ SMALL FEATHERED FRIENDS

Several large mammals have bird partners. Rhinoceroses, water buffalo, and other African land mammals are frequently followed by cattle egrets. These are white-feathered birds with long necks and long legs. As the mammals walk across a plain, they disturb insects in the grass. The insects fly up—right into the mouths of the watchful egrets. When the rhinos and water buffalo rest, the egrets hop onto their backs, where they feed on flies and other pests that are irritating to the mammals. The small brown-feathered tick-bird also helps mammals in this way.

The egrets also help the mammals by acting as sentinels. If they see enemies approaching, the egrets fly into the air. This warns the mammals of the danger.

Cattle egrets are natives of Africa. But early in the 20th century, some crossed the Atlantic Ocean to South America. Today they are found throughout the Americas. Instead of living with rhinos and water buffalo, they live with cattle.

Zebras and ostriches often live together. Each helps alert the other to the approach of enemies. The ostrich has excellent eyesight. This, together with its long neck, enables it to see enemies before the zebra can. The zebra has an excellent sense of smell. It may smell enemies before the ostrich can see them.

Another animal with a bird partner is the crocodile that lives in the Nile River. Its partner is the Egyptian plover. The crocodile is often bothered by leeches. Leeches are blood-sucking worms, and they attach themselves to the gums of the crocodile's mouth. When the crocodile spots a plover, it opens its mouth wide. The plover hops in and eats the leeches.

▶ LIVING WITH PLANTS

Some partnerships involve plants. Among the best known is that between bees and certain flowering plants. The bees visit the flowers to gather nectar and pollen. In return, they pollinate the flowers, thereby ensuring the formation of seeds. Without the flowering plants, the bees would starve to death. Without the bees, the plants would not be able to produce seeds. They would disappear from the earth.

Some species of hydra (tiny relatives of

Grenadier crabs carry sea anemones in their claws. If an enemy approaches, the crab thrusts the anemone into the face of the attacker, who must deal with the poisonous anemone tentacles.

Water buffalo have partnerships with cattle egrets and tickbirds. The birds hop onto the water buffalo's back and eat flies and other insects that irritate the mammal.

jellyfish) have algae living in their cells. The algae are protected from animals that might eat them. The benefit to the hydra is not known. But scientists have found that hydras with algae function better than hydras that do not contain algae. Perhaps the hydra needs the oxygen produced when the algae make food.

Sometimes an "outsider" benefits from a partnership. Certain ants in South America have a partnership with cecropia trees. The stalks of a cecropia tree contain many small chambers. Colonies of ants live in these chambers, and ants can always be found swarming over the leaves and other parts of the tree. One animal that loves to eat cecropia leaves is the three-toed sloth. As it feeds on the leaves, the sloth cannot help but eat some of the ants. These ants supply certain nutrients that the sloth needs. Without the partnership between the cecropia tree and the ants, the sloth might not survive.

The sloth is involved in some interesting relationships of its own. Green algae live in the sloth's fur, giving the animal a greenish color. This helps the sloth blend into its surroundings. Enemies are less likely to see a greenish sloth among the tree leaves than a brown sloth. However, too much algae can be harmful to the sloth. The algae population is kept under control by a small insect called the sloth moth. This moth only lives in the fur of three-toed sloths. It is provided with a good supply of food. And the sloth is provided with an efficient fur cleaner.

As you can see, animal partnerships involve all kinds of animals—and plants. They provide a variety of benefits: food, protection, camouflage, removal of parasites, and transportation.

Do people have partnerships with animals? What about the relationship between a person and a pet dog? Between a gardener and songbirds? Between a farm family and their egg-laying hens? Do you think both the people and the animals benefit from these relationships?

JENNY TESAR
Series Consultant
Wonders of Wildlife

These 12th-century Turkish cards had suits of coins, cups, swords, and clubs.

SUIT YOURSELF

You may be an expert at Crazy Eights, but did you ever notice that the red-suited kings' hair curls in, while the black-suited kings' hair curls out? Do you know which king has no mustache? Which picture cards are one-eyed? Many people enjoy card games, but few ever notice these details.

People have been playing cards for about 1,000 years, although no one knows for sure where the custom originated. Cards found in Turkey date back to the 12th century. The

Turkish cards were larger than the ones we use today, and they had suits of coins, cups, swords, and clubs. Similar cards appeared in Italy and Spain almost 200 years after the Turkish cards were made.

Cards then traveled to Germany and France. The invention of printing in Germany meant that cards no longer had to be hand painted. The Germans used suits of bells, leaves, acorns, and hearts. They still use these suits in special games. The French

German suits of bells, leaves, acorns, and hearts are still used today in special games.

were the ones who invented the suits we use today—clubs, diamonds, hearts, and spades. French cards became popular because of the simple shapes, and because the French decided that pictures were not necessary for most cards. The French simply used a stencil for all their numbered cards. This process was less expensive, and soon the French cards took over the market.

The French changed something else. The early European cards had been made only for the royal families, so they generally showed pictures of members of the royal court. But there were no queens in the decks. It seemed that card games were considered to be warlike contests, and women should not be a part of them. It was the French who introduced the queen. But even today, the Italians, Spanish, and Germans use a king and two jacks in some decks.

The French cards crossed the English Channel, and English cards were fashioned after them. Our modern deck looks much like the English cards of 200 years ago, picturing the costumes worn by 15th- and 16th-century English nobility.

There have been only two major changes in cards since about 1850. Before that time, the picture cards had shown the full figures of the members of the court. When the cards were dealt, people tended to turn them so that the heads were right side up. Turning the picture cards could reveal a good hand. The solution was to show only the head, at the top and bottom of the card. Thus cards do not have to be turned around.

The second major change was the corner index. The earlier cards had no corner marks, so a player had to have a hand spread wide to see all the cards. An opponent could easily catch a glimpse of the hand. With the corner index, all the important information about the card—suit and value—is printed in the corner. And a player can hold the hand tightly fanned. It may be that because the corner index shows the essentials of the card, most of us don't notice the details.

So the next time you play, take a closer look at the details. All the queens hold flowers, but one also holds a scepter. Which one?

J. R. BLOCK
Executive Director of Research and
Resource Development, Hofstra University

These modern muppet cards were made in Germany and show Kermit the Frog as king and Miss Piggy as queen.

CARDS AND THE CALENDAR

Here are some interesting comparisons between our modern deck of cards and the calendar:

The 4 suits could represent the 4 seasons.

There are 13 cards in each suit. While we have 12 months, the moon circles the Earth 13 times a year. These periods are called lunar months.

There are 52 cards in the deck and 52 weeks in the year.

If you count all the suit symbols on the face of the cards, in the corners, and beside the heads of the picture cards, there are 348. If you add 4 (for the number of suits) and 13 (for the number of cards in each suit), you get 365—the number of days in a year. You can even add the joker for leap year!

A MUSEUM FOR YOU

Would you like to climb down a manhole? Report today's news on television? Explore an attic in an old Victorian house? Work on an assembly line? You can do all these things in a day—at the Children's Museum in Boston, Massachusetts.

The museum opened in 1913, but it recently moved into a large 19th-century warehouse on Boston's waterfront. As you approach the brick and timber building, the object that first catches your eye is a giant milk bottle. The bottle is three stories tall and serves as a dairy stand where people can buy ice cream and frozen yogurt. It is also a reminder of the containers in which milk used to be packaged.

The museum takes up three floors in the building and has many exciting "hands-on" exhibits designed especially for children. These are some of the more unusual exhibits.

The Giant's Desktop is twelve times as big as a normal desktop. So is everything on it—telephone, pencil, paper clips, blotter, coffee cup, and ruler. You can walk on the desktop, jump up and down on the telephone's push-buttons, and even try to write with the huge pencil.

City Slice is a cross section of a city street. There's a traffic light you can operate. You can climb into a manhole and a sewer catch basin. From the outside, the brick-and-mortar catch basins look like large beehives. This kind of construction is no longer used. But such structures are still seen in older cities such as Boston. Also in City Slice are a car and a house that have been "sliced" open so that you can see how they have been put together.

Grandparents' House is a three-story model of a Victorian home. In the attic you can sew on an antique sewing machine. There are also trunks filled with old clothes for you to try on. Downstairs is a cozy parlor where you can read an old book or play a big old radio. In the kitchen you can discover how people cooked and washed dishes in days gone by. In grandfather's cellar you can use old tools.

The Japanese House is an authentic artisan's house and shop from Kyoto, Japan. It's a two-story structure that was built about 150 years ago. The house was taken apart, shipped to Boston, and rebuilt at the museum. It contains six rooms plus a bathroom, kitchen, and entry. There's a small garden complete with plants and statues. Special programs and exhibits held in the house teach visitors about life in Kyoto. For example, rotating exhibits explain how to make noodles, tatami (mats), shoji (paper screens), and pots. A colorful Children's Day festival includes folk dancing, kite making, martial arts demonstrations, and calligraphy.

What If You Couldn't? shows visitors what it's like to have a disability. You can get an idea of the problems faced by people who are unable to walk, who cannot see or hear, or who have learning problems or mental handicaps. For example, you can sit in a wheelchair and try to maneuver it over different kinds of surfaces. You can wear masks that decrease or completely block out your ability to see.

Factory lets visitors work at a company that makes spinning tops. First you punch in on a time clock. Then you join an assembly line. Your job may be to stamp discs out of cardboard. Or you may put a wooden peg through the center hole in each disc. Or you may be responsible for quality control. This means that you must check each top to make sure it's made correctly. Or perhaps you'll work for a while in the shipping department or the payroll office.

Work also lets you explore the world of jobs. You can work in a grocery store called the Congress Street Superette. Or you can work in the Health Care Clinic.

The Computer Center has twelve computer terminals. Visitors can play such games as tic-tac-toe, Hunt the Wampus, and Inchworm. "How's It Work?" is a program that explains how computers function. There is also an electronic "turtle" that navigates by computer commands.

Explore City Slice and see how a house is put together.

Visit Grandparents' House and try on old clothes in grandmother's attic . . .

. . . read a book in the old-fashioned parlor . . .

. . . and use old tools in grandfather's cellar.

KIDS FUN FACTORY

We're Still Here looks at the lives of New England's American Indians. It compares the way they lived centuries ago, when Europeans first came to New England, with the way they live today. Featured in the exhibit are a wigwam and a modern home.

At other exhibits in the Children's Museum, you can animate your own movies or use such tools as drills and lathes. WKID-TV is a news studio, where you can pretend you're a famous newscaster reporting a big story. Or you can operate a camera in the closed-circuit system. There are exhibits of dollhouses and toys. In a natural history corner you can watch common city animals such as mice, ants, worms, and cockroaches.

In addition to exhibits, the museum has a resource center where people can borrow books, games, audiovisual materials, and educational kits. Workshops are also held there. In one workshop, children dyed cloth using techniques developed in Nigeria. In another workshop they learned how to build a bird nest. In still another workshop they learned about Eskimo life. They examined fur clothing and hunting and fishing gear from the museum's collection. They learned how Eskimo people use dogsleds and snowmobiles. And they learned about the importance of storytelling in Eskimo societies.

The museum also encourages visitors to recycle materials in creative ways. Museum workers collect things that factories throw away—wood, foam, paper, and plastic parts. These odds and ends serve as raw materials for arts, crafts, and science projects.

In a place like the Boston Children's Museum, people have lots of fun and learn many exciting and useful things. It's a wonderful place to spend a day.

Walk into the recycling room, where all kinds of throwaway items are collected and reused.

THE KINETIC SCULPTURE RACE

Some look like insects. Some look like birds. Some look like amusement-park rides. And some look like nothing anyone's ever seen. But they all move, and they all take part in a strange race in Ferndale, California. It's such a strange race that no one even cares who wins. The official name of this event is the Ferndale Kinetic Sculpture Race. ("Kinetic sculpture" is sculpture that can move.)

In one recent race, four young people, whose ages ranged from 3 to 12, piloted a very strange machine. Made mostly of metal pipe, it looked like a red dinosaur skeleton on wheels. They called their vehicle Inch-by-Inch, probably to describe how it progressed down the street. By pushing and pulling at various parts of their contraption, they made it move. Inch-by-Inch won three awards: best artistic design, best mechanical design, and best all-around machine.

Entries in the kinetic sculpture race come in all shapes and sizes. Anything is liable to show up, but no engine-powered devices are allowed. Human energy alone must supply the power, and no driver's feet may touch the ground. One device, the Bubblemobile, was a huge wheel festooned with balloons. Like a hamster on an exercise wheel, the driver ran around the inside of the vehicle, and this motion made the Bubblemobile roll down the street.

The race has taken place every Mother's Day since 1969. And it all began as a joke. In that year, a Ferndale metal sculptor named Hobart Brown took a look at his son's tricycle and decided it was ugly. So he added some decorations and a few more wheels and wound up with a tall, wobbly thing that he called the Pentacycle. ("Penta" means "five." It had five wheels.) This was truly a kinetic sculpture—part art, part vehicle.

As Hobart Brown was working on the Pentacycle, a neighbor said that he could make a better kinetic sculpture. "That's a challenge!" Hobart said. "Build it, and we'll have a race on Mother's Day, right down the center of Main Street, Ferndale!" Soon other people heard about the race and they started fashioning kinetic sculptures, too. Word spread. And on race day, about a dozen kinetic sculptures showed up to race, and thousands of spectators were there to take part in the fun. Hobart Brown's Pentacycle did not win that first race. The grand prizewinner was the Tortoise, a giant turtle made of papier-mâché. It could shoot water and emit steam out of its mouth. And every

Human energy supplies the power to move these kinetic sculptures: Inch-by-Inch . . .

now and then the Tortoise "laid" a polka dot egg that rolled out the back.

After all the excitement, Hobart Brown realized that there would have to be another kinetic sculpture race the following year. And so the Mother's Day tradition began. And year by year, some very strange rigs have turned out for the race. Their names may give some idea of just how strange they are: the Silver Wing Velocipede, Powered Flower, Yellow Submarine, Tyrannosaurus Rust, and the Rickety Chickadee. Few of these machines go very fast. They aren't easy to steer and they often break down. To give an idea of how slow some go, one rule states that to win a prize, a vehicle must finish the three-block race within two hours.

As if a three-block race weren't long enough, a new race was added in 1974—a three-day, 34-mile (55-kilometer) event. It's called the Great Arcata to Ferndale Cross Country Kinetic Sculpture Race. This big race includes a difficult passage over sand dunes and treacherous crossings of Humboldt Bay and the Eel River. The machines in this race not only have to roll, they have to float as well. Among the entries in recent races were such mechanical marvels as the Gossamer Clam, the Double Trouble Mobile, and the Nervous Breakdown. And, just as in the Mother's Day race, no one really cares who wins. It's all done for the fun of it!

. . . and the Bubblemobile.

. . . the Double Trouble Mobile . . .

GLITTERING GLASS

You can make your home sparkle by creating these glittering glass objects—plates, bowls, jars, and bottles. And because you work with waterproof paints, your creations will last and last, even if they are washed over and over again.

Buy inexpensive glass plates and containers. Or use jars, bottles and other glassware that originally held various foods and liquids. A group of empty mayonnaise jars can be turned into a canister set. A wine bottle can become an attractive container for vinegar —or a vase for flowers. Baby food jars can become serving containers for mustard, ketchup, and relish.

The best paints to use are acrylic paints, which are waterproof once they dry. But other types of waterproof paints can also be used. Ask the salespeople in your local craft or art supply store what they recommend. Buy a selection of several colors: red, yellow, green, blue, and perhaps black and white.

It's best to plan your design before you actually begin painting. On a sheet of paper draw the outline of the object you are going to paint. Use colored pencils or felt-tip pens to sketch a design. The complexity of the design depends on your skills as an artist. But you don't have to be a master painter to create attractive objects. Anyone can draw stars or happy faces or funny fish.

Instead of making your own designs, you can also copy interesting designs from books or magazines. The plates shown here are decorated with Pennsylvania hex designs. The designs have special meanings. The star and tulips stand for faith and happiness. The sun and raindrops are for a large, healthy crop.

Any item can be personalized. For example, you might make a set of cereal bowls for your family. In the center of each bowl—or around the side—paint the name of a person in the family.

Once you have your design down on paper, tape it on the inside of the plate. The design should face the outside, or bottom, of the plate. Turn the plate over and simply paint the design, just as you paint within the lines in a coloring book. This method can also be used for bowls, jars, and for bottles with necks wide enough for you to put your hand into. When you cannot use this method, you will have to paint your designs freehand.

One thing is important: Do not put the paint on the side that will touch food. For example, paint the outside of a bottle or jar. Paint the bottom side of a plate or bowl.

Here are some tips:

1. Wash the glassware very well. The glass must be clean or your painted design won't stick to it.

2. Dry the glassware very well.

3. Avoid touching the painting surface. You do not want to leave fingerprints. It is best to handle the glass with tissue paper.

4. Keep a damp piece of tissue paper or a paper towel handy as you paint. If you make a mistake, wipe the paint off immediately, before it has a chance to dry.

5. Let the paint dry thoroughly. If the colors aren't as dark as you would like, apply a second coat.

Thousands of life-sized soldiers and horses were found in the tomb of the first emperor of China.

TREASURES OF ANCIENT CHINA

When the first emperor of China, Shi Huang Di (Shih Huang Ti), died in about 210 B.C., he did not go alone into the afterworld. He was escorted by more than 7,000 soldiers and horses.

The soldiers and horses were not real. They were made of clay. But they looked real. They were life-sized, and each was individually modeled and painted in vivid colors. Great attention was given to the soldiers' facial features, hairstyle, clothing, armor, even the soles of their shoes. The horses were also very accurately portrayed.

These magnificent figures were hidden in the emperor's tomb for more than 2,000 years. Their discovery, in 1974, was one of the most amazing archeological finds ever made. Nothing like the statues had been seen before.

Now people outside China have a chance to see some of the figures. An exhibit traveling through the United States in 1980–81 includes six soldiers and two horses, as well as

many bronze and jade objects. The exhibit, which is called "The Great Bronze Age of China," includes works from five major periods in Chinese history—the Xia (Hsia), Shang, Zhou (Chou), Qin (Ch'in), and Han dynasties. (Shi Huang Di, the first emperor, unified China and founded the Qin dynasty.) These periods span China's Bronze Age, which lasted from about 1700 to 100 B.C.

In most Bronze Age cultures, bronze was first used mainly for tools and weapons. But in China the metal was used chiefly for containers that held food or wine. It was used only by rulers and nobles because it was too precious to be used by ordinary people.

The containers were used in religious rituals, to hold offerings that were made to a person's ancestors. Each ancestor required different offerings, at different times of the year. And when kings or other important people died, their vessels were used in the funeral ceremonies and left in the tomb.

Some of the bronze objects are very sim-

The intricate vessel (*left*) and fierce-looking rhino (*above*) were made during the Zhou dynasty.

The elaborate elephant (*above*) and ceremonial ax (*below*) were made during the Shang dynasty.

ple. Others are extremely elaborate, their surfaces completely covered with designs. Animals are often part of the designs. Some of the animals are abstract; you have to look closely to see them. Other animals are portrayed much more realistically—it is easy to recognize tigers, elephants, and birds, as well as imaginary beasts such as dragons.

One particularly wonderful container is shaped like a rhinoceros. Its surface is decorated with an intricate scroll design that was originally inlaid with gold. Another container is shaped like a small elephant with a long trunk that curves up in the shape of a dragon. Its body is decorated with abstract patterns and animal forms.

Some of the vessels have inscriptions that record events in Chinese history. These are among the earliest written records of what happened in China long ago.

The exhibit also includes some jade objects made during the same time period. Jade was the most highly valued stone in ancient China. It was used for knives and ornaments.

All these Bronze Age objects have greatly increased our understanding and appreciation of the cultures of ancient China.

INDEX

ILLUSTRATION CREDITS
AND ACKNOWLEDGMENTS

14 Joe B. Blossom—Photo Researchers
15 Alpha; Russ Kinne—Photo Researchers
16 Gary R. Jones—Bruce Coleman, Inc.
17 Leonard Lee Rue III
18 Schmidecker—FPG; John Serrano—©1979 Photo Researchers
19 L. W. Walker—National Audubon Society
20 Barry Tenin; ©Porterfield-Chickering—Photo Researchers; Danish Ministry of Foreign Affairs; Phil & Loretta Hermann; Virginia Department of Highways and Transportation
21 Tom Stack & Associates; ©Porterfield-Chickering—Photo Researchers; Tom Stack & Associates; ©Mario Fantin—Photo Researchers
22 ©1980 David Olson—Black Star
23 ©1980 Douglas Kirkland—Contact; Ralph Perry—Black Star
24 ©1980 Walt Disney Productions
25 ©1979 Walt Disney Productions; ©1980 Walt Disney Productions
30 Jenny Tesar
32 ©Joan Lebold Cohen—Photo Researchers
33 Allan Power—Bruce Coleman, Inc.
34 ©Joseph Van Wormer—Bruce Coleman, Inc.
35 Jeff Foott—Bruce Coleman, Inc.
36–Courtesy Jananne
37 Lassetter
38 Sid Bernstein—Photo Researchers
39 Philip Jon Bailey—The Picture Cube

40 The Shelburne Museum, Shelburne, Vt.; The Shelburne Museum, Shelburne, Vt.; Abby Aldrich Rockefeller Folk Art Center, Williamsburg, Va.
41 Abby Aldrich Rockefeller Folk Art Center, Williamsburg, Va.; ©Guy Gillette—Photo Researchers
42 ©1980 Roger Sandler—Black Star
43 Steve Liss—Liaison
44 UPI
46 Michèle McLean/Pamela Carley Petersen
49 William Hubbell
50 What's to Eat and Other Questions Kids Ask About Food, U.S. Department of Agriculture
53 UPI
58–©1978 William Hubbell
59
60 The Granger Collection
62 Michèle McLean
63 Liaison
66 Barry E. Parker—Bruce Coleman, Inc.; ©1977 John Deitz—Photo Researchers; ©Chesher—Photo Researchers
68–Peter D. Capen—Terra
69 Mar Productions
71 Courtesy Wanderer Books
72 Courtesy General Motors; Courtesy Ford Motor Company
73 Oliphant ©1980 Washington Star
75 Courtesy Gulf & Western
80 Thomas Zimmermann—FPG
81 Focus on Sports
82 Paul J. Sutton—Duomo
83 Steven E. Sutton—Duomo

84 UPI
85 Hans Paul-Lehtikuva—Photoreporters; Lehtikuva—Photoreporters
86 Tony Duffy—Duomo
87–Don Morley—Duomo
88
89 Michèle McLean
90–Courtesy of Scholastic
93 Photography Awards, conducted by Scholastic Magazines, Inc. and sponsored by Eastman Kodak Company
94–Joseph Szaszfai—
95 Collection of Joseph and Edith Kurstin
96 Michèle McLean
97 H. Peter Curran—the Forbes Magazine Collection
102 Courtesy Advertising Council, Inc.
103 Courtesy U.S. Census Bureau
106 ©Soames Summerhays—Photo Researchers
107 ©Robert C. Hermes—Photo Researchers
108 ©Kjell Sandved—Photo Researchers
109 ©1973 Norman R. Lightfoot—Photo Researchers
110–Dr. J. R. Block
111
112–Steve Rosenthal
115
116–Vince Streano
117
118–Michèle McLean
119
120–The People's Republic of
121 China